TREES OF LIFE

OUR FORESTS IN PERIL
Second Edition

By Brian E. Stout

Table of Contents

Introduction

Why should you buy a home? We all want a home whether it is a condominium with minimal upkeep but a place to hang our hat after a long day at work or a trip around the world. Women want a home as an anchor. A place of safety, warmth and comfort. Men, take that away and your woman will fly! Not a sexist remark. A psychological statement. Women, ponder this thought.

Home is where the heart is. And yes, you can rent a home but there is always that degree of impermanence. Home is a place where memories are made, children grow up and come back to. These are a few reasons to buy a home. Make your own list right now before we start.

Why I want to buy a home:

What is keeping me from buying a home?

Homeownership has many advantages including:

<u>Equity Build-Up</u>

Making a monthly mortgage payment serves as kind of a savings plan. Over time, you build "equity" in your property that can be borrowed against with a HELOC (Home Equity Line of Credit) or converted into cash when you sell (profit for sale). Tenants paying rent *never* have the opportunity to build equity.

Sound Investment

Over time, your house can significantly increase in value, making it one of your best investments. It can also make it possible for you to move up to a larger home.

Tax Advantage

You will hear people touting about homeownership as a tax advantage. As a tax preparer and financial advisor, I want you to know that unless you itemize your deductions, this is not an advantage. You will need to have a cumulative amount on your Schedule A which is greater than your personal deductions on your 1040 in order to have this as an advantage. For the First-Time Homebuyers I work with, this does not apply.

Security and Satisfaction

Homeownership offers security of knowing you own your home and typically keeps your housing costs stable. Owning a home is the American Dream.

While it may seem that housing costs are simply too high for many people, sometimes it's an even greater risk not to buy. The same house that you can purchase today may cost you much more in the future due to inflation and rising interest rates. In addition, in order to retire, you'll need to build up enough savings and investment to generate yearly income of 70% of your pre-retirement income – a tall order without the capital you can acquire through home ownership.

If you've been thinking of purchasing a home within the next three to six months, you may have some concerns about your ability to buy. You're not alone – many people postpone buying a home for various reasons. The most common reasons include lack of a down payment, insufficient income and credit problems.

This handbook will address these issues and help start you on the path to homeownership.

Ways to Accumulate
A Down Payment

Before we buy anything, we need to know how we will pay for it, whether it is a car, clothing, anything! A house is not different. It is just the single most expensive item most of us ever purchase. Just like when you open a credit card, they want to know that you have a record of paying back and on time. Put yourself in the place of the bank/lender. They are lending you thousands if not hundreds of thousands of dollars so they want to make good and sure that you are in a position to repay the loan and that your record shows you have a willingness to pay your creditors.

Take a look at your spending habits- what you owe and if you pay on time. Even if you have a lot of debt, start organizing your bills and making a plan to pay them down or even pay them off.

There is good debt and there is bad debt. Other than a home, perhaps a car payment that fits your budget, the rest of your "high interest" debt is bad debt. Credit will be covered in more detail a bit later.

One of the biggest problems facing potential homebuyers today is coming up with enough money for the down payment and closing costs. The amount of money you have available can greatly limit or increase your purchasing power.

There are options alternatives to actually saving the money yourself. If you qualify, there are loan programs such as FHA, VA and community grants and loans that can help with low and even NO down payment.

This does not mean you do not need to have money in reserve. While qualifying you, the bank wants to know that you have "reserves" to pay not only your mortgage payment, but taxes and insurance as well.

Once you find the home and your offer is accepted, you will need money to submit with your offer, known as "Earnest Money". In a sellers market, you need to put a chunk down to have your offer considered.

Ernest money goes toward your down payment. This gets credited back to you at closing as part of the down payment. Meanwhile it becomes part of your offer and is held by a real estate company or an attorney, in what is called an "Escrow Account". It cannot be used for anything or anyone until you either buy the home or it is paid back to you if you decide not to move forward or cannot move forward within the confines of the agreement.

What does it cost you to get started? You need earnest money to make an offer. Once your offer is accepted you need a credit card to pay for the appraisal and for the home inspection. **These all 3 come out of your pocket within the first ten days of making an offer that is accepted**.

But Reserves and Earnest Money are not the only "cash" you need. At closing, there are costs involved. Depending on your loan and the lender there are costs for title insurance which the lender requires, with an option for an additional policy for the buyer. The attorney needs to get paid. There are taxes that will be paid upfront depending on what time of year you buy. Homeowners Insurance is required. These, to name a few, are some of the expenses you can expect at closing, even if you don't have to make a down payment. These are "closing costs".

How do you come up with the money to close? You have earnest money, you have inspection, you have appraisal… and then you have closing costs. What if you are that financially set? Read on.

Below are some additional resources that are acceptable to most lenders for closing costs:

1. Have your parents or an immediate family member give you money as a gift. Documentation will be required to prove that the money is actually a gift and not a loan. Any taxpayer is permitted to gift up to $16,000 per year (check to make sure the amount is current. It has increased regularly over the years) to another person without having to pay a gift tax. Technically, your mother could gift you $14,000 and your spouse $14,000. Your father could do the same. This would give you $42,000 for a down payment and closing costs. Check with your lender to see what the parameters are for your loan.

2. Borrow against your 401K or insurance policy. You can also cash out your 401K but you will be subject to withdrawal penalties, payment and taxes. You can use your 401(k) to buy a house without penalty, provided you use a 401(k) loan rather than a withdrawal. Unlike a 401(k) withdrawal, a 401(k) loan is not subject to a 10 percent early distribution penalty from the IRS. The money you receive will not be taxed as income.

3. Sell or borrow against an asset. Selling an asset such as a car can help increase the amount of money you have available. Borrow against an asset is also acceptable as long as you qualify with additional debt.

4. Obtain a low point or zero-point personal loan. This will reduce the amount of your closing costs substantially. A credit card offer at a zero or low rate is **not** acceptable.

5. Ask the seller to pay for all or part of your non-recurring closing costs. Your real estate agent can assist you with this when you make an offer on a home.

6. Ask the seller to carry back financing. If the seller does not need all of the equity in their property, they may be willing to carry some of the financing which will reduce the amount of your down payment.

7. Check into the city and/or county down payment assistance programs.

8. Close escrow late in the month to reduce the amount of prepaid interest on the loan.

9. Use the equity in another property if you own another home you are not selling by getting a home equity loan.

What Type of Credit is Needed to Buy a House?

Your Credit Report

Your credit score tells a lender a lot about your financial background. It is a report card about your behavior in the "School of Money." Any boo-boo's will follow you for at least 5 to 7 years.

Lenders draw from the three top reporting agencies and will use the middle score as your "number." It is a three-digit rating of your quality as a borrower. If high enough, you get the loan. Preferred rating is 680 or above, lowest rating (without issues) can be in the low 600's. And there are some lenders out there that will do into the 560's but they usually find a reason to not write the loan.

This takes into account your credit features such as the number of open credit cards and accounts, how close you are to your credit limits, how you repay or have repaid your credit. Especially tell-tale is how many 30,60,90 day late payments you have over the past 24 months. Late payments can kill a loan right up front. They also like to see how you have handled your available credit. Keep your balances below 30% of your available credit to keep your scores up.

Ways to Improve Your Credit Score

Needless to say, you need to pay your obligations on time. Your debt-to-income ratio will also be a key factor in qualifying for a mortgage. The front ratio will be your housing expense ratio compared to your income. The back-end ratio calculated total debt, including housing, credit card bills, student loans, car payments, etc. compared to how much your monthly income is. You can do the math on this yourself and see where you can cut down your debt. Student loans payments are currently calculated at 0.5% of the loan amount for FHA and 1% for conventional.

With your credit card payments, always pay BEFORE the due date (a few days before is fine) and always pay MORE than the minimum payment to best satisfy your creditors. Hopefully you pay your cards off in full every month due to the high interest they carry, but if you can't, then pay some extra beyond the minimum amount due. These tricks help keep you "under the radar" of being "strapped".

Pre-Approve Before You Buy

You should not pay to get pre-approved, nor should there be a fee to apply for the loan. Many lenders will apply "Junk Fees". These can and should be avoided. When you close, the lender may apply a processing and underwriting fee. Also there may be points (which will equate to dollars) to get your rate. These are discussed later. All of these are normal charges that apply to the closing costs.

Many people shop rates. Rates are rates because they are determined by "the powers that be". They are the same everywhere. Deviations come from the rate you qualify for based on your financial picture, and on a particular loan. Rates vary from FHA to conventional loans to buying your rate down, meaning that you pay for that lower rate in points. The difference in 1/8 of a point or a quarter of a point is insignificant in your monthly payment. The monthly payment is what is important to you, the Buyer! Even if you have bad credit and can get the loan, take it! You can remedy your credit and refinance even after a few months if it makes sense.

Before you begin searching for your new home, you need to determine how much you can afford. You may be able to afford more or even less than you think due to what the lender is willing to lend you based on your income and the amount of down payment you have. By getting pre-approved before looking for a home, you'll save time, energy and frustration because pre-approval:

- **Determines How Much Home You Can Afford**: Pre-qualification helps you avoid buying less house then you can afford or being disappointed if you don't qualify for as much as you had hoped.

- **<u>Shows You What Your Down Payment Will Be</u>**: You'll know approximately how much money you'll need for a down payment and closing costs.

- **<u>Lets You Know What Your Monthly Payment Will Be</u>**: You'll have a general idea of what your monthly principal, interest , taxes and insurance (PITI) payment will be.

- **<u>Identifies the Loan Programs You Qualify For</u>**: With the wide variety of loan programs available, it's important to know which types you qualify for and which best suits your needs.

At this point, the lender also can help you determine alternatives and strategies that could help you buy the home of your dreams. These may include:

- Special first-time homebuyer programs

- Low down payment programs

- Home rehabilitation programs

In order to get a "pre-approval" which most RE Agents require nowadays, your lender will need to know the following:

1. Your employment history and income

2. Your monthly debt and obligations. This will come in the form of a credit report which they will request to pull. Note, a pull from a mortgage company will not harm your credit score.

3. The amount and source of cash available for a down payment/closing costs

After a brief phone discussion during which the loan officer will ask you some general questions about your income, debt, assets, this information will help him/her determine the best type of loan for which you qualify. The loan officer will then study your information and if you qualify will issue you a "pre-approval" letter to give to your RE Agent. This letter will make your offer strong when you find the home on which you wish to make an offer.

How to Increase Your Purchasing Power

There are several factors that lenders take into consideration when determining how much they will lend to you for your home purchase. The three most important factors are your income, debts and down payment. Any one of these factors can greatly impact the amount of mortgage you qualify for. Lenders are primarily concerned with the percentage of your gross monthly income that goes to your new monthly housing expense and your new monthly housing expense plus your other monthly debts. As a general rule, no more than 28% of your gross monthly income should be going towards your monthly housing payment and no more than 36% of your income should be going to your housing payment plus other monthly debt. These guidelines vary by the amount of down payment you make and the loan program you choose.

If you have been pre-qualified and are not satisfied for the amount you qualify for, we have listed four of the most common obstacle to qualifying for a home loan below and some possible solutions to each.

1. **Excessive Debt:**

    a. Consolidate your debts by taking out one loan and paying off your bills with your money.

    b. Pay off long term debts by using some of your cash and making a lower down payment

    c. Selling an asset to pay off bills is another option

2. **Limited Income:**

   a. Income from alimony, child support, bonuses, overtime or future raises might be considered in qualifying.

   b. If you have overlooked any income be sure to tell your loan officer

   c. Find a co-mortgager who is willing to go on the loan with you to help you qualify

   d. Make a higher down payment

   e. Consider a financing option that will allow you to stretch your purchasing power, some of these options include FHA loans, adjustable rate mortgages, balloon financing or a graduated payment mortgage

3. **Credit Problems**

   a. Repair your credit file by contacting creditors and requesting that negative information be removed

   b. Pay off outstanding judgment liens and collections

   c. Re-establish good credit

4. **Lack of a Down Payment**

   a. Get a gift from an immediate family member

   b. Ask the seller to carry back financing

   c. Sell or borrow against an asset

   d. Borrow against or cash out your 401(K)

   e. Ask the seller to contribute towards closing costs

   f. Obtain a loan point or zero-point loan

   g. Consider financing options with low down payments

The Loan Approval Process
Your Real Estate Professional

Using a Real Estate Agent

If you are purchasing a home, it costs you absolutely **nothing** to be represented by a professional, licensed agent. An agent will work on your behalf to

- identify properties to suit your specifications
- schedule appointments to gain access to show
- advise you on price
- Negotiate the deal for you
- Monitor activities for you such as
  - o Home Inspection
  - o Needs your lender may have
  - o Review the Closing Disclosure with you
  - o Advise you of contacts for utility services

On behalf of the agent, loyalty is king. A great deal of work is done on your behalf by the agent and money is spent before the agent every gets paid.

 Even if you go to a new community, make sure to take the agent with you.

The person working for the builder represents the builder. Your agent will be your very own advocate and can negotiate upgrades, accompany you on walk-throughs (very important) and be of other benefit on things you may not have thought of.

You've taken the first step towards home ownership by selecting a professional real estate agent. You couldn't have made a better decision than to choose a realtor to guide you through the challenging home buying process. You can be assured that you that you will receive the best service with far less hassle and worry. Your real estate professional:

- Helps you assess your wants and needs to find the perfect match between what you can afford and the home that best suits your needs.

- Keeps your personal style in mind when selecting properties to show you

- Accesses all the properties for sale in your desired area by computer. "For Sale" signs and newspaper ads are not always a true reflection of everything that is on the market. Your real estate agent always knows what is available at any given time.

- Negotiates for you. Once you've found the home you want your Realtor will write up an offer and present it to the seller. This gives you the best opportunity to have your contract accepted.

- Gets the right price. Your Realtor is a specialist in your area and knows the market inside out so you will get the best price possible.

- Allows you to make your own decision. A professional agent works for you and respects your opinion. They will not try to force into a decision you don't feel comfortable with.

Table of Contents

I dedicate this book to my wife. Iris, and sons, Michael and Kurt, who provided much-needed support throughout my career in the Forest Service as we moved throughout the United States on 15 different assignments.

With this book I am passing my concerns to our four grandchildren to expand on the development of wisdom through observation and understanding of the complexity and importance of Nature.

A special thanks to those who encouraged and assisted me in this effort, "Doc" Smith, and Gordon Galloway. A very special thank you, to Dr. Melinda Kreth, whose help proved invaluable in the completion of this effort.

Preface

After completing the first 12 years of my education in 1956, I found myself struggling with what the future held for me in the business world. I suspect, like most other young people, my initial thoughts were to find a career path that would lead to affluence and the "good life." Two of our Western cultural values, greed and domination, were hard at work, and I was convinced all I had to do was pick a profession that was in demand and offered opportunities for a high salary. For the next two years I struggled to identify what my real purpose in life might be.

I think everyone starts by thinking about how to achieve financial success, and I was no exception. My father was a professional forester, so I was quite sure I needed to be different and could find a more lucrative occupation. During the second year of college, I realized that financial security was only a small part of the equation and that each individual has been endowed with unique talents and interests, which, if developed, can lead a person to find his or her role in our complex society. I do believe in the orderly creation of this world and that humans have been given the responsibility to contribute to the health and maintenance of our complex society and our natural environment. The satisfaction of success can be realized when one accepts his or her role and responsibility and begins to contribute to the well-being of the overall human environment. In 1958, I decided I had found my niche and transferred to the School of Forestry at the University of Minnesota. My interest in nature proved fertile, and I found forestry an exciting field of study. Upon graduation from college in 1960, I immediately started a challenging 34-year career with the U.S. Department of Agriculture, Forest Service.

From the very beginning of my professional experience, I had a haunting feeling that something was missing at the time from the application of forestry principles. For some reason, I felt like there should be more to the management of forested lands than just

1

extracting renewable natural resources. I cannot explain from where these concerns arose or why these concerns kept growing within my thoughts. As time progressed, I kept asking people I worked with why certain stands of trees were being harvested or why particular harvesting methods (silvicultural techniques) were being used? What were the objectives? The answers seemed to indicate the objectives were simply to meet specific targets for the production of forest resources. In contrast, I had always felt that forests were more than just storehouses of goods and services. They were more than just a supply of wood products, recreation experiences, or homes for a wide variety of wildlife species.

In 1964 I presented a paper at the Mid-West Wildlife Conference on work I was doing in the Mark Twain National Forest in southern Missouri. The paper presented an overview of a project I undertook to identify and collect site-specific data on individual forest stands on a 200,000-acre Willow Springs, Ranger District and to determine how this data could be used to analyze and develop site specific methods for managing these stands. The project provided the emphasis for me to begin to observe the complexity of the individual stands and lead me to define them as "communities."

Time and experience intensified my questions and concerns, and I developed an intense interest in how other cultures relate to nature. I began to search for opportunities to discuss my concerns with Native Americans. These discussions validated my sense that Western European cultural values and beliefs influence—perhaps even drive—scientific and technological processes in the United States. My final assignment in 1984, as Forest Supervisor of one of the largest National Forests in the continental United States, helped clarify for me the constraints that continue to cause inadequate management of our remaining forests. An invisible shield seems to overpower our science, technology, and common sense, a shield composed of some questionable but traditional Western European values upon which the United States was founded. These values include conquest, domination, and a quest for wealth and affluency.

Recently, I have come to believe that to complete my purpose in this life, I am obligated to express my concerns by writing this book.

I hope that by sharing my experiences and thoughts, I might open some eyes and minds to opportunities that will sustain and improve our valuable forests in the future.

Introduction

For centuries the forestlands on our planet have been valued for the renewable natural resources they provide. Seldom have I encountered professionally educated forest scientists who view our forests as individual communities involving complex relationships that support the requirements of most living organisms and creatures. Most foresters refer to cover types that cover vast acres of forested lands and then move on to the economic feasibility of resource removal opportunities. The demand and value of these natural resources have dominated the utilization of forests since the North American continent was first discovered. The exploitative mining of the continent's renewable natural resources started hundreds of years ago with the arrival of the first European explorers and later, settlers. For the first 200 years or so, the extraction of valuable resources took place with virtually no restrictions or regulations. These new settlers brought with them their European values and beliefs that, from our modern perspective, seem to have been based on greed and included a desire to conquer and dominate the "new world." Many of the explorers and settlers saw the vast forest resources as theirs by divine right to use as needed.

By the end of the nineteenth century, a few conservation-minded individuals finally recognized the need to consider managing responsibly our renewable natural resources. Before this time, the United States had been growing and developing with the hard work of the new European settlers (and their slaves) and their recognition of the abundance and value of the natural resources forests could provide. The forests were widespread and stretched beyond anything one could imagine; the horizons were almost literally beyond human comprehension. New settlers had been arriving weekly, and forest products were needed for shelter, protection, fencing, heat, and even food; many people actually saw the forests merely as obstacles that needed to be cleared to make room for crops and livestock. The new

5

European settlers set out to conquer the entire continent. By the mid-1800s the concept of American expansion was expressed as "manifest destiny," a phrase first used in 1845 by John L O'Sullivan in an article entitled "Annexation." Many people, including government leaders, subscribed to this belief.[1] Manifest destiny was a "belief in expansionism, American exceptionalism, romantic nationalism, and the natural superiority of people of English descent."[2,3]

The new settlers cleared the land and harvested and mined the resources required for the development of a new life on what they perceived to be a land of opportunity. The desire to develop and control this new land drove these settlers with a zest seldom seen before, and the need to conserve or manage these natural resources was likely far from anyone's thoughts. The indigenous people whom the settlers encountered were also viewed as obstacles that had no legal claim to the land, because written documentation of ownership did not exist. The new settlers laid claim to the land and began mining the natural resources for their own use and economic benefit.

However, by the late 1800s, a few conservation leaders, such as Bernard E. Fernow and Gifford Pinchot, appeared on the scene and began stressing the importance of managing our forest resources so that we might continue to provide needed forest resources to build our homes and communities in the future. Vast acres of public domain lands still existed in the western United States, and some people concluded that if properly managed, those forests could provide wood products for generations to come. These conservationists envisioned the management of our forests being similar to the management of farm crops only on a much larger scale and over a longer time period.

Early conservation leaders like Fernow and Carl Schenck looked to Europe, our homeland, for assistance, because forestry practices had been in place there for centuries. But the truth was that, even with its long history of forest management, Europe's population had expanded significantly and the continent had been experiencing a serious shortage of natural resources since the early 1400s.[4] America's need for forestry education forced us to turn to the

European academic institutions and ignore the forest resource problems that Europe had been experiencing for the last 400 years. Pinchot and any others interested in the forestry profession attended universities in France and Germany to study forest management and to further their understanding of forestry principles and concepts. This European education obviously influenced these early foresters and was instrumental in the development of education programs in the United States.

In addition to the academic principles and concepts of forestry, the Western cultural beliefs of control and domination were embedded into the new "science" of professional forestry. Forestry in Europe was viewed as an agricultural process involving the planting, growing, harvesting, and replanting of trees. The belief was that this cyclic process, if properly applied, would lead to a "sustained yield" of forest products for generations to come. The principle of "wise use" would later become the foundation for the forest management concept adopted by the U. S. Department of Agriculture, Forest Service. In fact, the Forest Service is an agency within the Department of Agriculture primarily because forestry was considered closely associated with farming practices. For years the German forests, managed by their "Forest Meisters," had been held up as prime examples of proper forest management. They were known for their neat appearance, with almost every twig being removed and used for some purpose. Citizens enjoyed free access to the forests and harvested numerous food items in addition to wood products. Unfortunately, European population expansion and resulting resource shortages were not adequately recognized.[5] European forest scientists probably should have been challenging much sooner the concept of "wise use" and "sustained yield."

Even though the policies of wise use and sustained yield helped push the United States into the world leadership position, I believe these management concepts are insufficient to properly manage our forests today. Forest management is far more complex than simply growing trees or even recognizing the multiple resources on each acre. Forest science must involve recognizing, studying, and understanding all the biological relationships among individual forest communities. We cannot accept anything less. The ability to predict the consequences of proposed management actions must become commonplace.

Most of America's early trained foresters either came from Europe or were educated in European universities and academies. To this day, U.S. colleges and universities provide forest management degrees primarily focused on understanding and managing the forest resources. Even though most forestry schools now require course work in ecology, I have observed little if any change in actual forest management, by recent graduates during my career. In fact, I submit that today's management of the National Forests in the United States has fallen behind as a result of increased pressure from preservationist-minded groups that became much more active since the 1960s. The aggressive road-building programs associated with the commercial removal of forest products from our remaining forested lands appeared to be the issue that triggered much of the new pressure to reduce timber harvesting and oil and gas exploration on public lands. I accept that many significant improvements have been added to forestry education curricula and that specialization in soil science, hydrology, landscape architecture, range management, wildlife biology, etc., is producing highly skilled resource scientists today. The addition of courses in ecology and environmental studies has broadened the knowledge base for our current resource professionals. However, my review of the major forestry school catalogs clearly shows that the focus remains on the study of resources from the forests rather than forest-ecology relationships and interactions. The mission statements I reviewed clearly define the course of study as preparing graduates to manage the renewable natural resources from the forests. The School of Forestry at Michigan Technological University defines forestry in its catalog as "the art and science of managing forest resources." The public forestry agencies and organizations and the private timber harvesting corporations remain focused on what we can take from the forests rather then what needs to be done for the forests to ensure our human environmental requirements of the future.

In 1905 the U.S. Department of Agriculture, Forest Service was established as a federal agency responsible for the management of vast acres of forestlands in America. Today, the agency oversees 191 million acres of public forestland and an additional 2 million acres of other public lands for a total of 193 million. The agency's motto became and still is "wise use" or "conservation," based on the management concepts learned in and observed from the European forestry schools.

Today, more than 100 years since the establishment of the U.S. Forest Service, we have learned much. Experience has taken us through the lessons of sustained yield, wise utilization, multiple-use plans, forest plans, and years of management experience. Unfortunately, little has changed in management application. My personal experience and continued interaction with current U.S. Forest Service employees confirm that, as a Nation, we continue to focus on the individual resources and view our forests as individual trees waiting to mature for harvest only to be replanted to provide a sustained yield for future generations. We apply broad-scale prescriptions to large forest types, plant acres of single-age, and single-species trees, and in some cases non-indigenous species, yet we fail to recognize the environmental consequences of these actions. Today's Forest Service employees spend the vast majority of their time writing reports, preparing environmental documents, and meeting assigned targets rather than actually visiting, analyzing, and developing management prescriptions for the very forest communities they are responsible for managing. A major part of their time is spent behind a desk rather in the field applying the scientific knowledge of their profession.

Despite the industrial demands of World Wars I and II as well as the consumer demands during the post-war eras, by the late 1960s, the preservation movement reemerged from its roots in nineteenth-century Romanticism, challenging established conservation principles. Much of the new emphasis on preservation was triggered by increased concern over increased forest-road access projects and a wide acknowledgment of human-caused environmental degradation. This movement has had a significant impact on reducing the amount of forest products from American forests, requiring the United States to import much-needed forest products from other countries. Many of today's building products come from Canada and other foreign counties. This reduction in harvest levels in America's forests has resulted in a lack of treatment for thousands of acres of forests, thereby allowing significant increases in insect and disease outbreaks as well as wild fires. I believe the preservation concepts for managing our forests (let nature take her course without human interference) are just as insufficient as the current conservation concepts (wise utilization of the resources). The human effects on the environment over the past 200 years have been severe and will require human intervention in the form of active forest management to correct.

My years of experience in forest management and active participation in numerous planning efforts with the Forest Service have led me to conclude that major change is needed in the current concepts of forest management. No longer can we simply study and manage the trees and other renewable resources of the forest. We must recognize that our forests are complex mosaics of living communities—changing daily—and essential to the survival of human life on this planet. Natural resource scientists responsible for managing our remaining forests must develop skills to recognize and understand these individual forest communities and the complex relationships within each community. A friend, "Doc" Smith, professor emeritus at the School of Forestry, Northern Arizona University, describes this skill as the ability to "read the land." Only with this insight will we acquire the necessary scientific knowledge to predict and assess acceptable and unacceptable consequences of proposed forest management actions and make the required adjustments in managing our remaining forests.

Chapter 1:
The Forestry Dilemma

The forests that currently cover the surface of our planet play a key role in sustaining human life. In fact, most living creatures, including humans, could not survive if it were not for our remaining forests. Forests are the main storehouse for carbon dioxide, produce life-sustaining oxygen, scrub our atmosphere of the human-induced toxic pollutants, and provide most of our required clean water. The value of our forests became abundantly clear on July 5, 2007, when the USDA, Forest Service published its report entitled, "Report on Abuse." The report stated that a single tree can absorb carbon dioxide at a rate of 48 pounds per year and release enough oxygen into the atmosphere to support two human beings for one year. It further stated that an acre of trees absorbs as much carbon dioxide in one year as the amount produced by driving a car 26,000 miles. This report concluded that over a 50-year lifetime, a tree generates $31,250 worth of oxygen, provides $62,000 worth of air pollution control, recycles $37,500 worth of water, and controls $31,250 worth of soil erosion.[6] Science suggest that at least 70 percent of the earth's land animals and plants live in forests and could not survive the destruction of their forest homes.[7] The USDA, Northern Research Station states that the majority of the U.S. drinking water supplies originate on forested lands.[8] Research by leading weather meteorologists and climatologists has shown that forest cover affects our climate significantly and the loss of forest cover is driving many of our climate changes.[9] Forest soils remain moist and productive due to the protection of the sun-seeking tree cover. Trees help propagate the water transformation cycle by returning moisture to the atmosphere through the process of transpiration. Without trees, many formerly forested sites have reverted to barren deserts.[10] Forest canopies block the sun's rays in the daytime and hold in heat at night. Thus, the removal of trees can disrupt temperatures causing extreme fluctuations harmful to plants and animals.

Historical records indicate at least 50 percent, and possibly as much as 70 percent, of the earth's land surface was once covered with forests.[11] Today, less than 30 percent of the world's land surface remains covered by forests.[12]

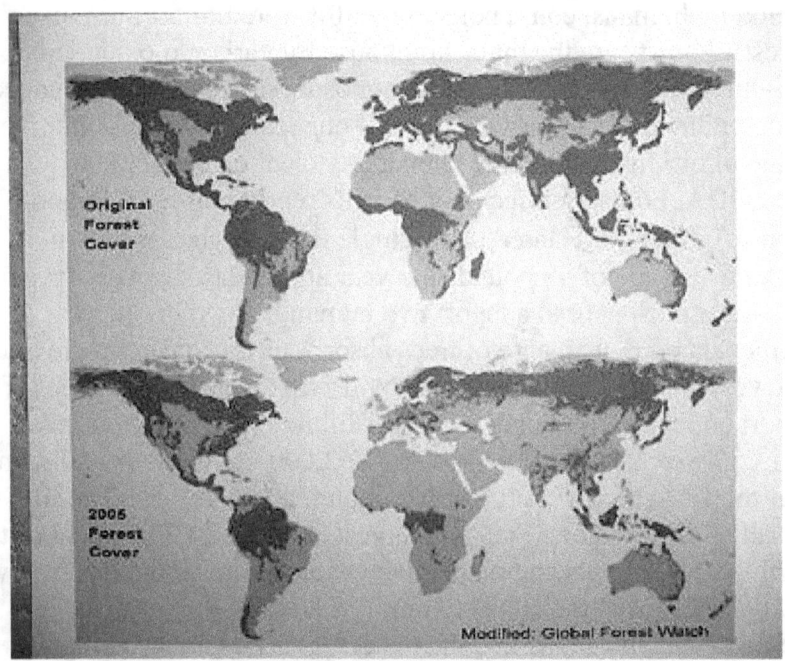

Original worldwide forest cover distribution compared to remaining forest cover in 2006.

Loss of forest cover is largely the result of deforestation by humans, which has been occurring at an alarming rate for years.[13] The rate of deforestation has slowed somewhat in recent years but is still progressing at an unsustainable pace. Scientists today predict that at the current rate, our tropical rain forests could completely disappear within the next 100 years.[14] We must also consider that the human population is growing at an explosive rate; it is currently seven billion and increasing at 78 million per year.[15] As our population expands, our demands on the remaining forested lands will intensify. Herbert Girardet, in his publication, "Save the Forests, Save the Planet" stated, "Never has the planet been more in need of forests. […] Never have the forests been under greater pressure than they are today."[16]

Deforestation has been occurring for many years, and our only hope is to slow the process significantly; otherwise, we will end up living on an Earth that may look and feel more like Mars. The deforestation process occurs for many reasons, but most are related to human demands. Urban expansion and the demand for forest products increase daily; however, the largest driver of deforestation is agriculture.[17] Clearing forestland to produce food crops and for grazing livestock is removing trees from millions of acres annually.

Land cleared for agricultural crops

Land cleared for grazing livestock

It is essential that we retain the remaining amount of forested acres; however, my focus will be on the management of our existing forests. My personal and professional observations indicate that, to maintain the health and vigor of much of our remaining forested lands will definitely necessitate active forestry management. What humans have desecrated will require help from our best scientists and managers to reverse. Old and diseased stands of trees cannot maintain the environmental requirements of other living creatures.

I was raised in the forestry profession, as the son of my father, a professional forester. My degree is in forest management, and my career included 15 different assignments with the USDA, Forest Service. During my career, I served in various positions in the four management divisions of the Forest Service: Ranger District, Forest, Regional, and National level. I had the opportunity to work with professional resource managers involved with the management of forestlands under public jurisdiction, private holdings, and large corporation ownerships. I also was fortunate to work with numerous natural resource educators and students on many forest and resource issues. During my career as a forester, these experiences raised concerns that have remained with me in retirement, concerns about the adequacy of our forest management principles and practices. I am troubled by the overriding focus on managing and extracting our forest resources rather than focusing on the health and condition of our remaining forestlands. For example, on a recent visit to Wyoming, I witnessed thousands of forested acres infested with a severe outbreak of pine bark beetle.[18] Most of the lodge pole pine trees, which made up 30–60 percent of the individual stands, were dead. The situation is an accident waiting to happen. Ignition at the wrong time will result in catastrophic fire that will destroy everything in its path, add major amounts of pollutants to the atmosphere, cause loss of life for many creatures—including humans—and cost millions of dollars to suppress. Yes, the stands will regenerate, but major changes will occur in the forest communities and among the multitude of relationships that currently exist in the ecosystem. The major question is: when will we finally begin to understand what the effects will be on the human environment? Would it not be better to understand the complex relationships and manage these communities to achieve a desired future condition that enhances the environment required of humans and other living creatures?

The problem that must be addressed is how to focus the management of our remaining forestland on the creation of healthy, vigorous, and diverse forest communities, so forests can maximize their biological contributions to the environment. I believe this will occur only if we are able to shift paradigms from a focus on extracting forest natural resources to recognizing and understanding the complex relationships within each forest community. Foresters have long recognized *cover types*, which refers to broad categories of similar trees. These cover types are then divided into stands of trees of the same species. When I use the term *forest communities*, I am referring to a unique living community consisting of diverse plants, animals, insects, and microorganisms, all of which are interacting with each other. Each community differs due to a variety of physical factors, such as soil type, altitude, climate, moisture levels, aspect (i.e., slope direction), soil depth, productivity, topography, etc. In addition to the physical characteristics, each community offers a different mix of living organisms. The ability to recognize these physical and biological differences provides the basis for identifying the individual forest communities.

I recognize that I am suggesting a renewed emphasis on *ecology*, defined as the scientific study of relations that living organisms have with respect to each other and their natural environment.[19] The word ecology was coined in 1866 by German scientist Ernst Haeckel (1834-1919). Modern ecology branched out of natural history, which flourished as a science in the late nineteenth century. Charles Darwin's 1859 evolutionary treatise, *On the Origin of Species*, is a pivotal cornerstone in modern day ecological theory.[20] Ecology is a sub-discipline of biology, the study of life.[21] Obviously, my focus on relationships in the management of our forestlands is not new and has, in fact, been a part of the scientific community for well over 150 years. Numerous articles and publications have presented volumes of data and theories on the subject since the late 1800s, yet little has changed in actual forest management as result of all this acquired knowledge. Why haven't things changed? Why have we refused to change our forest management goals of extraction and protection to the application of ecological principles to ensure healthy forest communities? Why do so many recently educated natural resource scientists continue to accept the emphasis on the management of individual resources from our forests rather than concerning themselves with the complexity of ecological relationships that exist within the communities they are responsible for managing?

Healthy community of mixed, second growth, northern
hardwoods with an occasional native white pine. Diversity
of tree species and age classes on a well-drained
southwest facing slope

To begin to answer these questions, we need to examine and understand current forestland ownership patterns. The motivation for owning forestland can vary with each individual owner, and "owners" can be corporations and governments, not just individual people. More than half of the forestlands in the United States of America are held by private corporations, groups, or individuals. In fact, in the United States, more than 56 percent of our remaining forests are held by private owners.[22] Various groups or individuals own these lands for a variety of reasons but usually for self-motivated economic reasons. Many forested acres are now held for private hunting preserves or for recreational purposes, because access to public forestlands is becoming more difficult as the population expands and the amount of public forestlands decreases. Timber-harvesting corporations have historically held large tracts of forestlands to support their wood product manufacturing business. Today, many of these large corporate holdings are being subdivided and sold to individuals for a variety of uses, including home development. It seems reasonable to conclude that most of these private landowners are motivated by economic considerations and would find it difficult to manage these forest communities for the noneconomic benefit of humankind.

We have recognized for years the problem of deforestation to provide land for agriculture, grazing, urban sprawl, and other land development purposes. To offset the impacts of these land-clearing programs, several efforts have been initiated to encourage the planting of trees on abandoned parcels of land. A major effort was made in the 1970s and 80s to encourage people to preserve or expand the number of acres of forestland through the "Tree Farming Program," a program that unfortunately focused largely on the value of forests for timber products. Now we must encourage private landowners to manage their forests for long-range ecological benefits, but their willingness to accept public needs will be strongly influenced by their ownership motivations.

Realistically, then, our attention must shift to the large public holdings of forestlands that are held in trust to benefit all humans. Why are professional foresters and other professional forest resource managers unwilling or unable to adjust the focus of managing our remaining forests from individual resources to creating healthy, vigorous, and diverse forest communities? And what do we mean by healthy, vigorous, and diverse forest communities? I am sure many forest scientists could provide a more detailed definition, but I look for a community composed of vegetative species indigenous to the location and site conditions; trees that are reasonably free of damaging insects and diseases and growing at optimal rates for the site productivity; and sites with a diversity of plant species, size classes, vegetation types, and a diversity of other living creatures indigenous to the area.[23]

I strongly believe that the most significant obstacle preventing us from seeing and accepting the opportunities for scientific changes and the need for new directions are our cultural values and beliefs. These values are creating an impenetrable wall that is blocking the vision of our forestry scientists and land management leaders from much-needed adjustments in forest management. The values that drive our science, in particular, forestry, are based on principles developed in feudal, medieval Europe.[24] European Feudalism first appeared in France and Germany in the 9th and 10th centuries. The impact that cultural values have had on science throughout history is not a new revelation, but I suggest it is somewhat new to the science of forestry. Many have tried for years to point out the significance that Western values and beliefs have played in the formation of scientific principles and practices. Lynn Townsend White Jr., a professor of medieval history presented a lecture in 1966 at the American Academy of Arts & Sciences titled, "The Historical Roots of Our Ecological Crisis," which was published the following year in the *Journal of Science.* He believed the Middle Ages were a decisive period in the genesis of Western technological supremacy and that medieval Christianity provided the "psychic foundation" of technological inventiveness.[25] He conjectured that the Christian Middle Ages were the root of the ecological crisis of the twentieth century. White, believed human relationships with the natural environment were dynamic and interactive, even in the middle ages. But he suggested that the mentality of the many people during the Industrial Revolution—especially the aristocracy and merchant classes—was that the earth was a resource for human consumption and that this view was based on medieval Christian attitudes toward nature as well as principles of domination, conquest, control, and greed (i.e., that God made the world for humans to conquer and exploit for their own needs).[26] It is true that today many religious scholars interpret the use of the word "dominion" in the Bible as requiring stewardship and caretaking. Unfortunately, the cultural values and beliefs of domination, conquest, control, and greed that have been passed down through years, are so overpowering and deeply ingrained in our society they have literally prevented scientists and engineers from implementing properly, the volumes of scientific principles and data surrounding the ability to observe and understand the complex ecological forest relationships required for future forest management. In other words, what we consider as our short-term needs and rights for an affluent life defines the goals for managing our remaining forests, rather than an emphasis on managing our forests to improve our chances for a supporting human environment in the future. Unless we change our emphasis from managing the forest resources to managing forest communities, we could double our scientific and technological knowledge base and still see limited change in the actual management of our forests. The solution can only be found in a new starting point for the analysis and development of forest management practices in the future. Our values must change to allow us to observe our surroundings and recognize the forest relationships that will be required for our future.

It is essential that we change our current forest management concepts and expectations. Leadership within our existing forest management institutions must establish new goals and objectives for managing our remaining forests. Current performance standards—which convey the desire of forestry leaders to continue focusing primarily on production of natural resources—must be adjusted. During my career I never encountered a situation in which a management unit or individual within the forestry profession was recognized for the number and quality of actual management prescriptions developed for individual forest communities in their area of responsibility. Performance standards that I did observe measured the number of resource outputs met, the ability to meet financial requirements, or the completion and accuracy of reports, plans, or other documents. Leadership must accept the responsibility for articulating goals and objectives that require quality management of our remaining forest communities.

Another major concern I have encountered is that forest managers believe their job is overwhelming due to the vast acres they are responsible for managing. I have talked with numerous forest resource managers who believe the intensity and extent of management I am suggesting is unreasonable due to the vastness of the forest areas involved. For example, a Forest Service Ranger District in the western United States may range from 400,000 to 750,000 acres. Typical staffing ranges from 15 to 50 people, and budgets are typically allocated on the basis of timber harvest levels, number of recreation visitor days, number of livestock grazed, etc. Even the budget process is rewarding the wrong things. We must envision our management responsibilities as starting with a requirement for sound professional forestland management prescriptions designed to maintain healthy forests and accept the fact that it is something we can and must accomplish. Our other Western value of a "can-do" attitude needs to be revitalized to allow us to change and accomplish this task.

Finally, forestland managers and resource scientists are completely overburdened with paperwork requirements. Reports, requests for data, and environmental documents demand so much time that there is little time to observe and manage the forest communities. Organizations have become so top heavy and bureaucratic that little time and few dollars remain for actual management of the forests. I have visited numerous Ranger Districts over the years and interviewed many young forestry and resource scientists within the Forest Service. I found most professionals spent no more than one day in ten actually in the forest. The majority of their efforts are spent behind a desk preparing environmental impact statements, planning documents, and budget requests along with other resource reports. While all these documents may be necessary, the problem is that while they meet the basic requirements of the law they are prepared with little direct knowledge of the forest communities and environmental relationships within them. Too many young foresters believe time does not permit us to collect adequate data for proper analysis of the communities. If you review their program of work and job standards, they are probably right. So we continue on our course of producing resource targets and fail in our responsibility to manage healthy and diverse forests.

Nobel laureate Daniel Kahneman in his 2011 book *Think Fast, Think Slow* provides an analysis of the human thinking systems that help us understand what is happening. Kahneman notes that the "think fast" system utilizes a great deal of intuition and, although less time consuming, can lead to inadequate and even wrong decisions. This system has been encouraged by government and industry management and to some degree by academia in an effort to improve productivity. In contrast, the "think slow" system relies on knowledge, observation, and understanding prior to a decision or action.[27] The "think slow" system is exactly what must be applied in the management of our forestlands.

So what happens if we don't make the necessary adjustments? Our forests and eventually the human species will suffer. Leadership must accept their responsibility for revising corporate goals, organizational structures, and performance standards that will support the positive changes required for future management of our forestlands.

Although I believe much of the problem with the current management of our forests rests with our forestland-managing organizations, our forestry academic institutions must also accept the fact that they have a responsibility to influence changes in their curricula that will assist in reorienting our forestry principles and practices. I recently searched the catalogs of more than a dozen of the top forestry colleges and universities throughout the United States and found each of them described their forestry programs as offering degrees in the management of "natural resources" obtained *from* forests rather than degrees in the management *of* forest communities and the intricate relationships that exist therein. Here are a few quotes from some of the forestry school program descriptions:

University of Florida, "A Program for Forest Resource and Conservation—

Forest Resource Management is for students seeking a comprehensive education in Forest Resource Science and Mgt."

Yale School of Forestry, "Preparation for a career in the

Management of Forest Resources."

Michigan State University, "Forest Resource Mgmt. Program, to provide the products and amenities that people want."

Michigan Tech. University, "Applied ecology and environmental science is the integrated study of the ecological, social and biotechnological aspects of Natural Resource conservation management."

University of Montana, "Goal—Knowledge, skill and understanding of Natural Resource Management and conservation."

This is only a sample of the forestry catalogs I reviewed, but it is sufficient to show that the focus still remains on the *resources obtained* rather than the health and vigor of forests ecosystems.

In reviewing the early history of the settlement of the North American continent, I found that the development of the science of forestry and examples of present forestland management reveals much about our Western culture and the overwhelming impact our values and beliefs have had on the science of forestry. It demonstrates how our Western values place humans in a dominant relationship with nature and discloses what I believe are opportunities for critical changes in the way we manage our remaining forestlands. I discovered that people in other cultures, including those of various Native American peoples, relate to their surroundings very differently. To appreciate academic and management changes that are needed, we must revisit our roots so we understand the development of our Western cultural values (i.e., medieval European cultural values), the historical harvesting of our renewable natural resources, the development of the science of forestry on the American continent, and current management of the acreage of forested lands that still remain.

Our Western cultural values have overwhelmingly influenced how we relate to each other and our surroundings and have provided the fundamental principles upon which forestry science and many other sciences have been based. These values include domination, conquest, extraction, and greed. Even though the concept of "conservation" "wise use" is steeped with these Western values, the management principles of "conservation" were, as we will see, a

22

significant step forward compared to earlier efforts to simply mine the resources without any management considerations. Prior to early management practices, our renewable natural resources were literally extracted as rapidly as possible to supply human demands and to provide economic profits.

What does all this mean for the future management of our remaining forests? We must accept that the value of our remaining forestlands far exceeds the value of the forest products that can be harvested.[28] Never forget that management is required and when properly applied, some level of forest resources will be the by-product of our management applications. The sustenance of human life on this planet may well depend on our ability to maintain and expand vigorous healthy forests.

The shrinking of our forests and the unhealthy state of many of today's forests are, I believe, a result of the greedy demands humans have placed upon them in the past. D. Henderson and L. Krahl in 1994 concluded in their publication, "Public Management of Federal Forest Land in The United States," that "the Forest Service continues to manage National Forests in a manner similar to that applied to aristocratic estates in feudal Europe."[29] I do believe the problems humans have caused or created for our forestlands can be resolved with proper management. This human assistance, in the form of intensified management, will require some significant changes in the way we view and relate to nature and our surroundings. Change will not come easily, but we do not need to reinvent the wheel.

Learning about and paying attention to different cultural values and beliefs can offer opportunities for realistic change. As philosopher Seyyed Hossein Nasr has stated, "the environmental crisis is fundamentally a crisis of values" and that "religions, being the primary source of values in any culture, are thus implicated in the decisions humans make regarding the environment."[30] Some philosophers have proposed that Eastern religions as well as those of indigenous peoples, neo-pagans, and others, have offered more eco-friendly worldviews than Christianity.[31] A review of the historical and current information on a variety of cultures that have occupied

23

and still exist on this planet reveals a wide range of ways these people relate to their surroundings, nature. This is particularly true when one compares Western and Eastern cultures. I have chosen to compare the two very different cultures that met on the North American continent about AD 1500 because I believe they offer a meaningful comparison of how different cultures relate to their surroundings and to each other. These two cultures had very diverse values and related to their surroundings very differently, thereby providing an opportunity to examine how these differing values might influence the science of forestry. An in-depth study of many other cultures and their views of relationships with nature is recommended. My focus will continue on the two cultures that met face-to-face on the North American continent more than 400 years ago. I recently heard a Native American express his relationship to the earth by saying "I belong to earth." He saw himself as a small part of the great environment within which he lived. I immediately thought how my ancestors would have stated the relationship as "the earth belongs to us." We see ourselves as the dominant creatures for which God created this planet and its valuable resources. Lynn Townsend White Jr. argued that Judeo-Christian theology was fundamentally exploitative of the natural world because (1) The Bible asserts human's dominion over nature and establishes a trend of anthropocentrism, and (2) Christianity makes a distinction between humans (formed in God's image) and the rest of creation, which has no "soul" or "reason" and thus is inferior.[32]

The difference in the way Western culture and most Native American cultures view nature conveys a completely different outlook, and I believe the Native American views offer significant insights into opportunities for future management of our forestlands. The following quotes help convey the different ways in which Native Americans relate to nature compared to our Western beliefs. Walking Buffalo of the Stoney Tribe said:

"Did you know that trees talk? Well they do. They talk to each other, and they'll talk to you if you listen. Trouble is white people don't listen. They never learned to listen to the Indians so I don't suppose they'll listen to other voices in nature. But I have learned a

24

lot from trees: sometimes about weather, sometimes about animals, sometimes about the Great Spirit."[33]

An unknown Blackfeet Chief said, "The land was put here for us by the Great Spirit and we cannot sell it because it does not belong to us. … Only the Great Spirit can count the grains of sand and the blades of grass of these plains."[34]

Several years ago I came across a copy of a speech given by Chief Seattle of the Suquamish Tribe, in 1854. The presentation marked the transfer of the tribal lands to the U.S. government and the tribe's requirement to relocate to a reservation. The Chief's words were eloquent and for me encapsulated the differences between Native American and Western perspectives in a most profound way. The wisdom of this great Chief, captivated me and led me to an appreciation of how cultural values impact science. I have included Chief Seattle's words so we might benefit from his profound insight into the complexity of life and Nature and support why I feel this compelling need to adjust many of our Western values for future scientific endeavors.

Seattle

The only known photograph of Chief Seattle,
taken 1864

The Great Chief in Washington sends word that he wishes to buy our land.

The Great Chief also sends us words of friendship and goodwill. This is kind of him since we know he has little need of our friendship in return. But we will consider your offer. For we know that if we do not sell, the white man may come with guns and take our land.

How can we sell the sky, the warmth of the land? The idea is strange to us.

If we do not own the freshness of the air and the sparkle of the water, how can you buy them?

Every part of this Earth is sacred to my people. Every shining pine needle, every sandy shore, every mist in the dark woods, every clearing and humming insect is holy in the memory and experience of my people. The sap which courses through the trees carries the memories of the red man.

The white man's dead forget the country of their birth when they go to walk among the stars. Our dead never forget this beautiful Earth, for it is the mother of the red man. We are part of the Earth and it is part of us. The perfumed flowers are our sisters. The deer, the horse, the great eagle, these are our brothers. The rocky crests, the juices in the meadows, the body heat of the pony, and man—all belong to the same family.

So, when the Great Chief in Washington sends us word that he wishes to buy our land, he asks much of us.

The Great Chief sends word he will reserve us a place so that we can live comfortably to ourselves. He will be our father and we will be his children.

So we will consider your offer to buy our land. But it will not be easy. For this land is sacred to us.

This shining water that moves in the streams and rivers is not just water but is the blood of our ancestors. If we sell you our land, you must teach your children that it is sacred, and that each ghostly reflection on the clear water of the lakes tells of events and memories in the life of my people. The water's murmur is the voice of my father's father.

The rivers are our brothers, they quench our thirst. The rivers carry our canoes and feed our children. If we sell you our land, you must remember, and teach your children, that the rivers are our brothers and yours, and you must henceforth give the rivers the kindness you would give any brother.

The red man has always retreated before the advancing white man, as the mist of the mountains runs before the morning sun. But the ashes of our fathers are scared. Their graves are holy grounds, and so these hills, these trees, this portion of the Earth is consecrated to us. We know that the white man does not understand our ways. One portion of the land is the same to him as the next, for he is a stranger who comes in the night and takes from the land whatever he needs. How can you sell the sky, the warmth of the Land? The idea is strange to us.

The Earth is not his brother, but his enemy, and when he has

27

conquered it, he moves on. He leaves his father's grave behind, and does not care. He kidnaps the Earth from his children. He does not care. His father's graves and his children's birthright are forgotten. He treats his mother the Earth and his brother the sky as things to be bought, plundered, sold like sheep or bright beads. His appetite will devour the Earth and leave behind only a desert.

I do not know. Our ways are different from your ways. The sight of your cities pains the eye of the red man. But perhaps it is because the red man is a savage and does not understand.

There is no quiet place in the white man's cities. No place to hear the unfurling of the leaves in spring or the rustle of the insect's wings. But perhaps it is because I am a savage and do not understand. The clatter only seems to insult the ears. And what is there to life if a man cannot hear the lonely cry of the whippoorwill or the arguments of the frogs around a pond at night? I am a red man and do not understand. The Indian prefers the soft sounds of the wind darting over the face of the pond, and the smell of the wind itself, cleansed by a midday rain, or scented with the pinon pine.

The air is precious to the red man, for all things share the same breath—the beast, the tree, the man they all share the same breath. The white man does not seem to notice the air he breathes. Like a man dying for many days, he is numb to the stench. But if we sell you our land, you must remember that the air is precious, too, that the air shares its spirit with all the life it supports. The wind that gave our grandfather his first also receives his last sigh. And the wind must also give our children the spirit of life. And if we sell you or land, you must keep it apart and sacred, as a place where even the white man can go to taste the wind that is sweetened by the meadow's flowers. accept, I will make one condition; the white man must treat the beast of this land as his brothers.

I am a savage and do not understand any other way. I have seen a thousand rotting buffaloes on the prairie, left by the white man who

So we will consider your offer to buy our land. If we decide to shot them from a passing train. I am a savage and do not understand how the smoking iron horse can be more important than the buffalo we kill only to stay alive.

What is man without the beasts? If all the beasts were gone, men would die from a great loneliness of spirit. For whatever happens to the beasts, soon happens to man. All things are connected.

You must teach your children that the ground beneath their feet is the ashes of our grandfathers. So that they will respect the land, tell your children that the Earth is rich with the lives of our kin. Teach your children what we have taught our children, that the Earth is our mother. Whatever befalls the Earth befalls the sons of the Earth. If men spit upon the ground, they spit upon themselves.

This we know. The Earth does not belong to man; man belongs to Earth. This we know. All things are connected.

Whatever befalls the Earth befalls the sons of the Earth. Man did not weave the web of life; he is merely a strand of it. Whatever he does to the web, he does to himself.

But we will consider your offer to go to the reservation you have for my people. We will live apart, and in peace. It matters little where we spend the rest of our days. Our children have seen their fathers humbled in defeat. Our warriors have felt shame, and after defeat they turn their days to idleness and contaminate their bodies with sweet foods and strong drink.

It matters little where we pass the rest of our days. They are not many. A few more hours, a few more winters, and none of our children of the great tribes that once lived on this Earth or roam now in small bands in the woods will be left to mourn the graves of a people once as powerful and hopeful as yours.

But why should I mourn the passing of my people? Tribes are made of men, nothing more. Men come and go, like the waves of the sea.

Even the white man, whose God walks and talks with him as friend to friend, cannot be exempt from the common destiny. We may be brothers after all; we shall see. One thing we know, which the white man may one day discover—our God is the same God. You may think now that you own Him as you wish to own our land, but you cannot. He is the God of man, and his compassion is equal for the red man and the white. The Earth is precious to Him and to harm the Earth is to heap contempt upon its Creator.

The whites too, shall pass; perhaps sooner than all other tribes. Continue to contaminate your bed, and you will one night suffocate in your waste.

But in your perishing you will shine brightly, fired by the strength of the God who brought you to this land and for some special purpose gave you dominion over this land and over the red man. That destiny is a mystery to us, for we do not understand when the buffaloes are all slaughtered, the wild horses are tamed, the secret corners of the forest heavy with the scent of many men, and the view of the ripe hills blotted by talking wires.

Where is the thicket? Gone. Where is the Eagle? Gone. And what is it to say goodbye to the swift pony and the hunt? The end of living and the beginning of survival.

So, we will consider your offer to buy our land. If we agree, it will be to secure the reservation you have promised. There perhaps, we may live our brief days as we wish. When the last red man has vanished from this Earth, and his memory is only a shadow of a cloud moving across the prairie, these shores and forests will still hold the spirits of my people. For they love the Earth as the newborn loves its mother's heartbeat.

So, if we sell you our land, love it as we have loved it. Care for it as we have cared for it. Hold in your mind the memory of the land as it is when you take it. And with all your strength, with all your mind, with all your heart, preserve it for your children and love it. As God loves us all.

One thing we know. Our God is the same God. This Earth is precious to Him. Even the white man cannot be exempt from the common destiny.

We may be brothers after all.

As I read these words presented almost 150 years ago, many thoughts came to mind. We labeled these people savages? Was it to justify the way we dominated and destroyed their way of life? Were they really savages or an intelligent society with different values and beliefs from our western society? I find great wisdom in Chief Seattle's words and opportunities to learn much as to how we might improve our relationship with Nature, our surroundings, our life-sustaining environment.

Comparing the Native American and European cultures demonstrates the importance of studying values in formulating scientific principles and provides opportunities to search for new and better ways to manage our life-sustaining forests.

Most people recognize that our Western values have put the United States in a position of world economic leadership. We enjoy the most affluent lifestyle ever seen on this planet. Certainly drive, determination, and a strong work ethic have played major roles in our country's achievements. Education has also played a key role in our country's success. Science and technology for the management and extraction of natural resources have advanced to unbelievable levels. Unfortunately, the management of our forestlands has not focused sufficiently on understanding the long-range potential impacts of our resource extraction.

Other cultures, including many Native American cultures, appear to have a much more sensitive eye for observing the complex relationships within nature and individual forest communities. They lived close to nature, and their ability to observe and understand nature determined their very survival. They appreciate the necessity of maintaining a balanced relationship with their surroundings. Black Elk of the Oglala Lakota tribe expressed the Native American view:

"Perhaps the most important reason for lamenting is that it helps us to realize our oneness with all things, to know that all things are our relatives: then in behalf of all things we pray to Wakan Tanka that He may give us knowledge of Him who is the source of all things, yet greater than all things."[35] traditional Western values, and I believe suggest opportunities for change in future forestland management.

An appreciation of past Western cultural values and beliefs helps us understand the influence these values have had on the basic principles behind much of modern-day science, technology, and

These Native American views and outlooks differ greatly from education. Observing and analyzing the differences in value systems between various cultures may offer insights that can provide a more optimistic outlook for our future life. The discovery of the North American continent brought together two different cultures that see nature very differently. Listen as the Native American speaks and the words they use: Father Sky, Mother Earth, the teachings of grandfathers and grandmothers, the four-legged creatures as our brothers and sisters, even our brothers and sisters the rivers and the lakes. What do you hear? I hear a culture that is focused on family relationships, a culture that observes carefully and appreciates nature. I do not hear thoughts of domination or greed.

A review of the early European settlement of the North American continent provides an understanding of how domination, conquest, and greed drove the extraction of our natural resources, including forest resources. European settlers, the ancestors of most of us in the United States today, brought with them a set of values and beliefs that were rediscovered from many ancient civilizations and became dominant in the feudal medieval European time period.[36] These values must be given credit for capitalism, individual freedom, religious freedom, and a strong work ethic, which many of us cherish today. We must recognize that these Western values strongly support the concepts of dominance, conquest, development, power, wealth, and greed. Dominate society tends to believe that it is our God-given duty to force all who are different to adopt our ways and values.

Native Americans tend to view their relationship with nature and their surroundings quite differently from the rest of us. History and archeology have recorded the rise and fall of several great Native American civilizations over the thousands of years these populations have been known to exist, such as the Incas of South America, the Mayans of Central America, and the Aztecs of what is now Mexico. These were advanced civilizations by any standard, whose existence and demise still hold many mysteries to be uncovered. Modern-day Native American populations are made up of numerous groups known as tribes, and certainly there were differences in individual tribal values and beliefs. There are, however, some common values and beliefs that appear to be shared by Native Americans. Belief in the Great Creator (Father Sky), Mother Earth (the provider of sustenance) created by the Great Creator, life after death in the spirit world, living in balance with nature and all living creatures, and the sharing of possessions rather than individual ownership are common shared values.

The dilemma challenging management of our forestlands today is how to reorient the scientific thinking process away from the production of natural resources in the remaining forests to management of healthy forest communities. Forest scientists must focus on preparing detailed prescriptions for individual communities, and forest resources must be seen as by-products of this professional process. We can no longer continue to mine, nor ignore, our remaining forests. Human involvement in the form of professional management is essential and will require foresters who can literally read the land before proposing resource removal actions. It will require forest scientists with the insight to predict the results of proposed actions prior to implementation. Our goals and objectives must change. Our very existence may well depend on our ability to adjust our priorities for the management of our forestlands.

Chapter 2:
Settlement and Confrontation

Our European ancestors came to this continent in search of religious freedom, wealth, and opportunity. They were, for the most part, God-fearing believers who saw the valuable natural resources as provided by God and ours, by divine right, to use as we saw fit. They found the land itself unencumbered by titles or deeds, therefore available to the first to claim it. They believed that no one owned the land or the valuable resources that were abundant as far as one could see. They brought with them the European system of justice that holds the individual responsible for his or her actions, but they encountered indigenous peoples with a system of balance that was, and still is, foreign to many of us.

The European and Native American cultures and their values collided on this continent and provide a sharp contrast for analysis. To understand the overwhelming influence cultural values have had on our Western society, we need to recall the early colonization, settlement, and development of the North American continent by our European ancestors most often thought to have begun in 1492, although recent findings indicate European occupancy may have occurred long before.

Archaeological discoveries in the form of primitive stone structures suggest that European travelers might have arrived on the North American continent as early as AD 800,[37] and it is now accepted that the Vikings arrived at least as early as AD 1,000.[38] The legend of Saint Brendan, an Irish monk, involves a fantastic journey into the Atlantic Ocean in search of paradise in the sixth century. In fact, some very recent theories on Clovis technology have suggested that some of the Paleolithic people in North America might have come from southwestern France by way of the North Atlantic ice shield as much as 20,000 years ago.[39] Regardless of the accuracy of the early European visits to the new continent, [32, 33] it wasn't until after Columbus's discovery of the Caribbean Islands in 1492 that large numbers of European immigrants began arriving and permanently colonizing the new land of opportunity. European immigrants searching for a new life, wealth, and freedom set out to colonize this new continent and share in the conquest and development. Word spread fast about this land of opportunity, rich in natural resources and free to the first to arrive and claim it. There was no documentation indicating any previous ownership of this vast new world, even though there were large numbers of inhabitants living on the continent. The new arrivals believed they were free to claim as many acres as they needed to establish their homes, farms, and plantations. The indigenous people of this continent, at first, seemed friendly and willing to share, but the quest for land would soon change the friendly, sharing relationship the early settlers had with the Native Americans.

By the early 1400s the European population had grown significantly, and Europe was experiencing major shortages in renewable natural resources, including wood products.[40, 41] Competition for the land was at an all time high, and a few adventuresome individuals were beginning to discuss searching abroad for new opportunities and riches. This quest for wealth and the shortage of natural resources led Queen Isabella of Spain to finance an Italian, Christopher Columbus, to sail west in search of new opportunities.[42] Columbus thought he had discovered a new trade route to the markets of the East and Mid-East, but in fact had discovered a new continent. The continent was occupied by an indigenous people that Columbus named Indians.[43] Historians now estimate that at the time Columbus landed on the islands of the Caribbean, the North American continent was occupied by more than 1,000,000 Native Americans.[44] When the Spanish finally did reach the American continent, forests stretched as far as one could see, and valuable minerals, such as gold and silver, appeared to be abundant.

Later Spanish expeditions followed, such as those led by Hernán Cortés, Hernando De Soto, and Francisco Pizarro, searching for wealth in the form of gold and silver. They encountered the indigenous people, earlier labeled Indians by Columbus. These native people seemed to have little appreciation for the value of the precious metals that were so prized by the Spanish conquistadors. Stories suggest that during the 1500s, the Spanish were able to amass large treasures of gold and silver through barter, battle, and mining; however, careful review of historical records raises questions about the reliability of these stories.[45] Most of the Spanish effort was focused in what is today Mexico and the southern portions of the United States, including states such Florida, Texas, and New Mexico. Pizarro however, led his expedition to South America, primarily into Peru.

By the late 1500s, word had spread, and other Europeans especially the French, British, and Dutch, were developing an interest in exploring and colonizing the new continent. Soon boatloads of new immigrants were arriving almost weekly. The first settlements were along the northeastern seaboard of what later became the United States of America. These new settlers also encountered the strange native inhabitants of this continent and found them to be friendly, peaceful, and willing to share their food and their land. These Native Americans spoke a strange language and had no written documentation of land ownership, birth records, marriage records, death certificates, or other historical information. The concept of land ownership was unknown to them; in fact, a word for ownership did not even exist in the languages of these newly encountered people. How could you own something that was provided by the Great Creator? As Chief Joseph (Rolling Thunder) of the Nez Perce Tribe reportedly stated, "Sell a country! Why not sell the air, the clouds, and the great sea, as well as the earth? Did not the Great Spirit make them all for the use of His children?"[46]

To all the new arrivals, this land of opportunity appeared to be a dream come true. Vast, deciduous forests stretched as far as the eye could see and were teeming with a large variety of wildlife. The soils were rich, moist, and capable of growing needed crops for food. Land was free for the taking, and with hard work, one could begin a new life free from religious persecution and European tyranny.

The new settlers brought not only their hopes for a better life but also their domesticated livestock. Pigs, chickens, cattle, and horses were not indigenous to North America; they had been brought by early explorers and later by the hoards of settlers. These new domesticated animals frequently competed with native species for food and space and in some cases had a devastating impact on native animal species and on the Native Americans' way of life. The "balance of nature" they valued was about to be adversely affected by the new settlers, the introduction of nonindigenous species, and competition for the land itself.

Early settlers, at first, found the Indians very different in their ways of life but reasonably friendly, and most settlers established a peaceful relationship with many of the various Native American tribes. The celebration of the first Thanksgiving exemplified this early relatively peaceful coexistence. This relationship was short-lived however, as the competition for land became a major conflict. Native Americans believe they are a part of the land and living in balance with "Mother Earth" will sustain them and their way of life. One did not own Mother Earth. These lands had however, been their hunting grounds for thousands of years. The land of this continent did "belong" to them in a sense, and although they were willing to share, they would never give up what was rightfully theirs. The demand for the land was growing at a rapid pace, and a major conflict was inevitable.

The new European arrivals brought many changes, including sickness and disease completely foreign to the American continents and their inhabitants. Native Americans had no immunity to these diseases, and the results were devastating. In some cases, such as smallpox, large numbers of Indians in some tribes were wiped out. In fact, because the demand for land by new settlers had became so intense, it has been suggested that in a few cases Native American populations were intentionally exposed to some of these diseases in an effort to remove them from their tribal locations. There have been suspicions in American history that the military gave smallpox-infested blankets to some Indians in 1763. William Trent, commander of the local militia, wrote in his journal "Out of our regard for them (two Indian chiefs) we gave them two blankets and a handkerchief out of the smallpox hospital. We hope it will have the desired effect." Trent's journal has been taken as the major evidence for using smallpox-infested blankets, but it is definitely subject to a different interpretation. One can also interpret the gesture as one of gratitude. The interpretation is complicated by a letter dated July 16, 1763, from Lord Amherst to Colonel Bouquet in which Lord Amherst wrote, "Could it not be contrived to send the smallpox among those disaffected tribes of Indians? We must on this occasion use every stratagem in our power to reduce them." Regardless of the interpretation of the impact of Europeans settlement by the late 1700s, the Native American population had shrunk to an all-time low.[47]

The 1600s saw the establishment of the original 13 colonies in the northeastern part of America, and although the European settlers and Indians had lived a reasonably friendly coexistence for a limited time, conflict over the land was beginning to surface. Various types of marriage and family relationships between particularly European immigrant men and Native American women from some of the Eastern tribes were beginning to occur, and it seemed possible that a cooperative relationship might be possible. Sharing appeared to have some hope as new settlements were being established in the northeast part of the new world. The eastern Native American tribes worked hard at maintaining a peaceful relationship even though they felt threatened by the land-hungry settlers. European immigration was continuing to increase, and as the population grew, demand for land and resources expanded.

The new riches in America were attracting more and more immigrants from Europe, which was about to spark a major conflict between the new and indigenous cultures. One culture saw "Mother Earth" as a gift from the "The Great Creator" for them to occupy and share with other living creatures, believing that if one lived in balance with nature, Mother Earth would sustain life. The European newcomers saw the land as unencumbered, free for the taking, and capable of being manipulated and developed to provide for human needs, regardless of the costs to the land or the rest of the world.

They were accustomed to owning a parcel of land in fee title and documented with a deed. The Native Americans did not even have a word for ownership and they knew only the concept of sharing. When the new settlers began forcing the Indians to vacate their traditional lands and hunting grounds, the Native Americans viewed this as losing a part of themselves, their very souls.

These same greedy European values were applied to nature and its renewable natural resources. In their 1991 book *Native American Wisdom* Kent Nesburn and Louise Mengelkoch stated,

"The Native Americans shared a common belief that the earth is a spiritual presence that must be honored, not mastered. […] The western Europeans that came to these shores had a contrary belief. To them, the entire American continent was a beautiful but savage land that was not only their right, but duty, to tame and use as they saw fit."

The Western values of ownership and dominance came with the settlers, and by the 1700s had begun to create a conflict of major proportions. The new Americans laid claim to the land and created a legal system that documented their ownership of the land, including the surface and underlying resources. Efforts to drive the Indians from what they considered their territory and hunting lands led to conflict and eventually wars. After almost 100 years of living together, the settlers had learned little of the Native American cultural values or had rejected the values as uncivilized or old fashion. They knew nothing of or did not care about the Indian system of balance versus the settler's European-based system of justice. The concept of sharing the Great Creator's gifts was completely foreign to most settlers. The concept of Mother Earth providing and sustaining was replaced with the belief that "mother nature" could be manipulated and be [36, 37] forced to provide for their needs. Timber harvesting, grazing and mining became major industries. Large areas of eastern forested acres were being cut down to make way for agriculture, grazing, cities, and towns. Furniture manufacturing in the new land was in the developmental stages, and the demand for high-quality hardwood lumber was beginning to develop.

In 1775 the colonies went to war against Great Britain to gain their independence and freedom. The French and their Indian allies aided the colonists in their successful efforts. A new nation was formed in 1776, the United States of America. Victory over the British was proclaimed in 1783, and the focus went back to the development, domination, and expansion of this new nation. The conflict between the European settlers and the Native Americans intensified, and more tribes became involved in fighting for their territory as the white settlers began their push West.

By 1830 the white settlers could no longer tolerate Native Americans in the eastern United States. Congress initiated the "Removal Period." All Indian tribes occupying lands east of the Mississippi River were to be removed and placed on lands set aside for them in the West. Land was set aside as "Indian Territory," and several tribes were forced to relocate to the area that would later become the state of Oklahoma. Tragedies, such as the Trail of Tears, were initiated by the U.S. government. Many tribes tried to protect their hunting territory but were unable to stand up to the army of the United States. A few Native Americans were assimilated into the white culture, with the majority being removed to reservations or Indian Territory in the West.

The eastern United States was now open and available for development and domination by the white Americans. Cities were being built, resources devoured, and fortunes amassed. Many of the forested acres had been cleared and were now farms and plantations. The southern pines were being used to build homes, barns, stores, and other needed structures. Northern hardwoods provided the high-quality materials needed for furniture and other decorative items. The medieval European values of domination, conquest, and utilization had taken over the continent and the people who once occupied it. Throughout much of the modern Western history of the last 500 years, the European white Christian culture has dominated and required other cultures—people who are different—to change and adopt their ways and values or be pushed aside. These same cultural values and beliefs strongly influenced the way land and the natural resources were viewed. Nesburn and Mengelkoch in their book *Native American Wisdom* stated that, "as the twentieth century draws to a close, Western civilization is confronting the inevitable results of this European-American philosophy of domination." [48] They went on to compare the two different sets of values represented on this new continent: "The spiritual wisdom of the Native American is not found in a set of scriptural materials. It is, and always has been, a part of the fabric of daily life and experience."[49] The authors include a number of quotes from Native Americans that demonstrate the striking difference between Western values and Native American beliefs. For example:

Chief Seattle, Suquamish & Duwainish: "All things are connected. Whatever befalls earth befalls the children of the earth."

Tecumseh, Shawnee: "Indian faith sought the harmony of man with his surroundings, the white men sought the dominance of their surroundings."

Chief Joseph, Nez Perce: "We were contented to let things remain as the Great Spirit Chief made them. They were not, and would change the rivers and mountains if they did not suit them."[50]

The focus of our Western values was clearly articulated by John O'Sullivan in 1849 with the presentation of his concept of "manifest destiny." The quest to control, dominate, and conquer the land, its resources, and its indigenous peoples is what led to the Indian wars and the final removal by the late 1800s of most Native Americans from their traditional tribal lands.

* * * * *

My intent has not been to present a detailed historical review of the early settlement of the North American continent but to illustrate how two societies of people, with very different beliefs and values, relate to nature and their surroundings. I do not suggest one is "right" and the other "wrong," but if we are willing to open our eyes and minds, we can share and learn from each other. These two cultures that clashed on the North American continent offer an excellent example of how different people view their relationships with nature. I do believe the time has come when we must change our Western values that influence how we relate and manage our natural surroundings. My contention is that the basic values of a culture can and do create barriers that adversely affect science, engineering, and technology within the society.

Somehow we must move beyond the concept that the land and resources were placed here for our benefit and begin to literally see the forest rather than just the trees! The next chapter reviews the emergence of the science of forest management, so observe closely that the focus has been—and largely still is—on the natural resources obtained *from* the forests rather than the management *of* the forests themselves.

Chapter 3:
The Evolution of Forestry

The 1700s were the start of a period of rapid growth and development in the New World. There were homes, farms, and plantations to be built, communities to be developed, transportation systems to be established, and fortunes to be made. The discovery of the abundance of valuable natural resources was occurring rapidly. Opportunities appeared endless, and a man was only constrained by the amount of effort he was willing to put forth and the amount of time he was willing to commit.

By the mid-1700s, serious consideration was underway for the creation of a new free nation. The 13 colonies had developed individual governments, and the establishment of the Continental Congress took place in 1775. This Congress, located in Philadelphia, Pennsylvania, was essentially the government of the United States from 1775 to 1788. The Congress gradually took on the responsibilities of a national government. By June 1775 the Congress established a continental army as well as a continental currency.[51] In July of that year the Congress created a post office for the "United Colonies." On July 4th, 1776, bells rang out in Philadelphia indicating the Declaration of Independence had been adopted. In 1787 the Constitution of the United States was ratified, and the new nation was established. The foundation for the new egalitarian democracy was the Iroquois Federation. In fact, the principles of the federation were studied and used to help write the Constitution of the United States. The birth of the nation came into being as a result of military rebellion (what some today might call acts of terrorism), heroism, civil strife, political intrigue and treachery, and numerous clashes between defenders of the old order and supporters of the new.[52]

And so, with a zest seldom seen before, the settlers set out to build a new nation and, they hoped, share in the resulting rewards and riches. The abundance of natural resources would add much to this nation. Not only were there sufficient resources to meet the needs of the expanding population but the surplus offered opportunities for marketing and trading with European countries, thereby adding great wealth to the United States. Soon merchant ships were routinely sailing between the two continents. Furs, gold, silver, and other resources were being shipped to Europe, and more settlers were embarking to seek their fortunes in the United States.

The Extraction Period: ca. 1700–1850

The aggressive push for development initiated the *extraction period,* roughly 1700-1850. The eastern forests needed to be cleared to provide for farms and plantations. The demand for logs, lumber, fence posts, and fuel was expanding rapidly. Soon companies were being formed to meet this demand and to create wealth. Logging operations expanded and sawmills were built. Before long, the title "Timber Baron," referring to the wealthy developers of the timber industry, was instituted. These influential men played a strong role in the development of procedures and laws surrounding the extraction of lumber and wood products from the vast U.S. forests. As the eighteenth century drew to a close, the logging industry was looking to expand, and it was obvious that large fortunes were awaiting those capable of mining the vast virgin conifer forests of the West. To accomplish this would require the construction of new communities to house the labor that would be required to harvest and mill the seemingly endless old growth forests.

The extraction period also led to the discovery and demand for hard-rock and energy minerals, resulting in an aggressive exploration and mining effort. Copper was discovered in 1705 in Connecticut; 1748 brought the first coal mining; and in 1799 gold was discovered on the Reed farm in North Carolina.[53] Crude oil had actually been used by the Indians for centuries as a medicine and to waterproof their canoes and other objects. The first discovery of oil by the European settlers came in 1627 by a Franciscan missionary traveling near Cuba, New York. The first drilling for oil occurred in

1821 near Fredonia, New York, near the shores of Lake Erie. Soon thereafter, the global petroleum industry started in the Appalachian Basin of northern Pennsylvania.[54]

Driven by a passion for wealth and a desire for an affluent life, the new Americans were changing the face of the continent. The mining of our natural resources was undertaken at a feverish pace. The extraction period was in high gear! The uncle of Charles Alexander Eastman, a Santee Sioux Native American, stated, "The greatest object of their lives seems to be to acquire possessions—to be rich. They desire to possess the whole world."[55]

Charles F. Wilkinson in his 1993 book *Crossing the Next Meridian: Land, Water, and the Future of the West* presents an analysis that covers the extraction period and the overwhelming influence of developers and investors had on the formulation of law and policy surrounding the extraction of America's natural resources. He goes on to state, "these natural resources are governed by what I have come to think of as the lords of yesterday, which are laws, policies and ideas, not people."[56] Throughout his book, Wilkinson refers to the European Medieval value of greed and describes its strongly visible and obviously dominant role in the formulation of early U.S. policy and law. Wilkinson concludes that "the controlling legal rules, usually coupled with extravagant subsides, do not fit with the economic trends, scientific knowledge, and social values of modern day America."[57]

We must not overlook the extraordinary influence that natural resource extraction efforts had on the development and management of our forest and rangelands, but we must also recognize the influence our Western values and beliefs have had on the formulation of the laws and policies surrounding the principles of forestland management. Wilkinson suggests that "natural resources are more than amenities, they actually drive much of our Nation's economy." They drive the society intellectually and emotionally. The barons of industry (and now, baronesses, too) still wield strong influence on land and resource decision-making today. Wilkinson suggests, "that law and policy ought to be the manifestation of public will."[58]

The extraction period from 1700 to 1850 created massive wealth for the entrepreneurs and led to the establishment of the United States as a world financial power. The period also intensified many social problems. Greed, competition, and domination were responsible for the amassing of great wealth and rapid development as well as events that remain an embarrassing part of our history. The Native Americans' culture was nearly destroyed as they were literally forced from their homelands and their way of life. Slavery continued in the United States well after it had been banned in the British Empire, and Africans were enslaved and shipped to the United States to provide labor for the development of the nation. Individuals were murdered over mining claims, grazing rights, and land ownership. Yes, the extraction period was in full swing, and it brought out the best and the worst in the morals and cultural values of the new nation.

In 1849 John O'Sullivan presented his concept of "manifest destiny," which intensified the belief of people in Europe and the United States in the supremacy of the Western cultural values.[59] Many people, including government leaders, championed the concept of dominance and supremacy. The expansionists in the United States commonly invoked the name of God, arguing that He had placed these abundant resources here for a reason and that it would be contrary to divine will not to utilize the land and resources for productive purposes.

We must accept that our cultural values strongly dictate how we live, treat other people who are different from us, and manage our surroundings. It was these values from our European forbears that, on one hand, allowed us to achieve greatness, but on the other hand, led us to dominate and destroy anything that got in our way, including nature. The extraction period offers a detailed picture of our Western value system and our relationship with nature. It demonstrates a strong commitment to domination, conquest, unbridled development, and greed by the dominant society. Admittedly, vast individual fortunes were amassed during this period; however, there appears to be little appreciation for the adverse consequences from such avaricious attitudes and actions.

We have rationalized that we were simply carrying out our divine right to utilize what had been provided by God. The extraction of natural resources from our forests was accelerating, but not everyone was happy about what was happening during the extraction period. By the end of the 1840s concerns over excessive timber harvesting and deforestation was beginning to surface. In 1877 U.S. Secretary of the Interior Carl Schurz warned, "The rapidity with which our country is being stripped of its forests must alarm every thinking man."[60]

The Management Period: 1850-1905

By the end of the nineteenth century, a few individuals began to comprehend the need to manage our renewable natural resources to provide for the future. A new period, the *management period*, was about to blossom. It remains important to keep the Western value system in mind as it continued to dominate the formation of the scientific and management principles of this period. Understanding the overwhelming influence of cultural values is necessary if we are to understand and evaluate human actions and beliefs.

The first few years of the *management period* covers the 1850s and involves the first recognition of the need to begin placing some limitations on the removal of our renewable natural resources to provide for the future. Around 1870 a few dedicated individuals began an effort to get the United States to recognize that some type of management was required to provide a sustained flow of products from our forests for future generations. There is no need to present a complete review of the historical establishment of forest management on the North American continent, but delving into the history of some of the key leaders in the forestry movement establishes the evidence to support the overwhelming influence that Western values had on the development of forestland management principles.

The person considered to be the "Father of American Forestry" was Berhard E. Fernow. He was born 1851 in Hahensalza, Prussia, Poland.[61] His education included study at the University of

Königsberg in East Prussia and the Forestry Academy at Munden, Germany. He then immigrated to the United States. Fernow served as the first Chief of the Division of Forestry of the United States from 1886 to 1898.₆₂ During his time as Chief Forester, Fernow pushed for the establishment of National Forests and the introduction of forest management. Fernow's efforts led to the need for educated foresters.

France and Germany were known in the nineteenth century for their established academic programs in forestry, even though the continent had experienced 400 years of significant population growth and overutilization of essential natural resources.₆₃ Forestry was a new profession however, and in the United States none of our colleges or universities offered a forestry curriculum. If a person wished to pursue an education in forestry, he had to attend one of the European universities. As renowned as the European forestry programs were, the continent was still faced with major resource and financial problems as a result of past over utilization.

In addition to schools for forestry education, Germany had a long history of managing its forests and woodlots. Trained "forest meisters" were employed to manage the individual woodlots and forested timber tracks. The almost complete utilization and cleanliness of each woodlot was considered a sign of outstanding forest management. For decades, German forestry was considered by most to be the example to which all other forest management should strive to imitate. Finally, in 1898, Fernow resigned out of frustration as Chief of the Division of Forestry and became Dean of the New York State College of Forestry at Cornell University. This was the second educational forestry program to be established in the United States. However, the school closed in 1907, and Fernow became the founding Dean of the University of Toronto's Faculty of Forestry. He also served as the editor in chief of the *Journal of Forestry* until his death in 1923.₆₄

Fernow's influence and persistence finally got the attention of conservation-minded U.S. President Theodore Roosevelt. In 1893 Roosevelt set aside the first forest reserve, known as the Yellowstone Forest Reserve.₆₅ This reserve included portions of what today are the Bridger-Teton National Forest and the Shoshone National Forest. President Roosevelt's efforts in 1891 were the start of what today is 193 million acres of National Forest System lands.

Carl Schenck was another well-known leader in early U.S. forestry. He was born in Darmstadt, Germany, in 1868 and had looked to forestry as a career since his youth. Schenck graduated from the Institute of Technology in Darmstadt at 18 years of age. Two years later, he enrolled for graduate studies at the forestry school of the University of Geissen in Germany. Schenck completed his doctorate in 1895 and was recommended for a job in the United States working for George W. Vanderbilt, whose Biltmore Estate was located near Asheville, North Carolina, and included some 120,000 acres of mountainous forestland. The Biltmore Estate, which is open to the public, is known today as the "Cradle of Forestry" and has played an important role in the development of scientific forestry in America.[66] Carl Schenck became forester of the Biltmore Estate and implemented new scientific management and forestry techniques that had never before been applied to forests in the United States. In 1898 with permission from Vanderbilt, Schenck founded the Biltmore Forestry School on the estate grounds, the first forestry school in the United States.[67] The school offered a one-year study course focusing on *silvicultural theory*. Silviculture refers to the various techniques of harvesting and regenerating trees by attempting to copy nature's methods. Intermediate thinning, shelterwood harvesting, clear-cutting, and diameter-limit thinning are all timber-harvesting treatments designed to produce wood products, improve growth rates, and reestablish new stands of trees. From 1898 to 1909 the school provided education and hands on experience for many of the leading foresters of the time.[68] In 1909 after a falling-out with Vanderbilt, Schenck left the Biltmore Estate, taking his school with him. Schenck continued his emphasis on forestry education for much of the rest of his life. He traveled extensively to lecture on scientific forestry. In 1955 Schenck passed away, leaving a legacy that proved to be the foundation for forestry education in America.

One of the best known forestry leaders of the time was Gifford

Pinchot, born in 1865 in Simsbury, Connecticut. He graduated from Yale College in 1889 and went on to do postgraduate study at the French National School of Forestry in Nancy, France.[69] Upon his graduation, he returned to the United States and became an active leader in the forestry movement.

Pinchot's father had made a fortune from lumbering and land speculation but regretted the damage his activities had done to the forestlands. Conservation became a family focus, and Gifford was pushed by his father to become a forester. Gifford's wealth allowed him to pursue the goal of forest management concepts without worrying about making a living. In 1896 the National Academy of Sciences formed the National Forestry Commission and appointed Pinchot the director. With an endowment from Pinchot's father, Gifford and fellow Yale alumnus, Henry S. Graves, founded the Yale University School of Forestry in 1900.[70]

Pinchot's concepts of forestry set him apart from other forestry leaders in that he pursued a national vision for the management of the public forestlands. He sought to change the policy of dispersing public renewable natural resources to private holdings to a policy of maintaining public ownership and management. As a resource conservationist, Gifford frequently found himself in conflict with the timber companies, which he thought had no concern for the future, and with resource preservationists, who strongly opposed the commercialization of any of the natural resources. He thought both extremes were shortsighted and wrong. Pinchot's opposition to the preservation concept led him to undertake an aggressive effort to have the Forest Reserve lands moved from the Department of Interior to the Department of Agriculture.[71] This move may seem inconsequential, but it actually proved to be monumental in terms of forest management for the future. If these lands had remained under the management of the Department of Interior, we might be a very different country today.

Under the patronage of President Theodore Roosevelt, Pinchot managed to gain control of the forest reserves. In 1905 the Division of Forestry was established as a new agency within the Department of Agriculture, known as the Forest Service. Pinchot served as the agency's first chief from 1905 to 1910.[72] However, President William Howard Taft fired Pinchot in 1910 for speaking out against the president's polices and those of Secretary of the Interior, Richard Ballinger. Secretary Ballinger was an advocate of the preservation concept, which Pinchot vehemently opposed in favor of conservation. Pinchot's continued public attacks on the secretary finally led to Ballinger being forced out of office in what became known as the "Pinchot-Ballinger" controversy.[73]

This scandal, also known as the "Ballenger Affair," was a dispute about favoritism, kickbacks, and coal mining in the administration of President William Howard Taft. The firing of Pinchot led to a great deal of animosity between Taft and the Progressive (Roosevelt) wing of the Republican Party and started the split that eventually broke the Progressives out of the Republican Party to form the Progressive (Bull Moose) Party of the 1912 elections. This split in the Republican vote basically handed the presidency to Woodrow Wilson, himself a progressive Democrat. I find it interesting how history tends to repeat itself, for in 1980 James G. Watt was appointed the Secretary of the Interior. His tenure as secretary was controversial primarily from his perceived hostility to environmentalism and his endorsement of the development and use of federal lands by foresting, ranching, and other commercial interests. Secretary Watt, based on his Dispensationalist Christian beliefs, is attributed to have said, "After the last tree is felled, Christ will come back." Although there is some question as to whether Secretary Watt actually made this quote, it clearly demonstrates the continued conflict between the theories of "Conservation" and "Preservation" in managing our forestlands.

Gifford Pinchot moved on and founded the National Conservation Association where he served as president from 1910 to 1925. In 1920 the governor of Pennsylvania appointed him to the States Commissioner of Forestry. In 1923 he became the twenty-ninth governor of Pennsylvania and in 1931 was elected for a second term.[74] During his remaining years, he served as an advisor to Franklin Roosevelt and wrote a book about his life as a forester. Pinchot passed away in 1946 but will always be remembered for his leadership in the early development of the profession of forestry in the United States.[75]

Although Pinchot had several disagreements with other forestry leaders of his time, his concept of "wise use" still fits well with the early principles of forestry education and practices of forestland management. The entire profession was focused on the growing, harvesting, and replanting of trees. The concept of "conservation" is based on the premise that professional foresters, through protection, manipulation, and management, can grow trees as a farmer grows crops and provide a sustained flow of wood products from our forestlands.

The lesson that stands out is the strong influence the Western value system had on establishing our forestry education programs and forestland management principles. The focus on individual resources, trees, and the belief that it was contrary to divine will not to put the land and resources to productive use, confirms the cultural values of domination, greed, and control. Many of Pinchot's writings disclose his strong bias toward the European Medieval feudal forestry values. He stated, "It must be clearly borne in mind that all land is to be devoted to its most productive use for the permanent good of the whole people, and not to the temporary benefit of individuals and companies. […] The first duty of the human race is to control the earth it lives upon. […] The National Forests are to be used for utilitarian purposes, and timber production is the preeminent use. These lands existed for the benefit of the home builders first of all. […] The purpose of forestry, then, is to make the forest produce the largest possible amount of whatever crop or service will be most useful, and keep on producing it for generations of men and trees. […] To grow trees as a crop is forestry."[76]

This brief history of early forestry in the United States is presented only to establish the strong European influence on the profession and does not give adequate credit to the many others, particularly those in state forestry organizations, who made major contributions. However, this brief review clearly demonstrates the basic focus on the resources and trees as the foundation for the principles of professional forestry.

Observing and understanding the influence of cultural values is essential and forms the basis for challenging the current practices in the profession of forestry. The principles of European forest management, conservation, sustained yield, and wise use are inadequate to ensure our future. Preservation alone will also prove inadequate to ensure a healthy future for our remaining forests. A detailed understanding of forest community relationships is the only way to provide the applications of scientific forestry required to manage our forests in balance with nature and to recognize potential adverse consequences of proposed management actions.

Chapter 4:
Establishing the U.S. Forest Service

The review of the early development of the forestry profession in the United States clearly demonstrates the strong influence from European forestry principles and practices. Many of our ancestors obviously brought with them their Western values and beliefs from Europe, but our early forest managers also reached out to their homelands for assistance in their quest for information and knowledge. The review to this point has more than adequately demonstrated the dominant role cultural values and beliefs have had on the implementation of scientific and technological principles and applications and will become even more obvious as we review the establishment of the leading forestland management agency in the United States. Observing the development of one of the largest public forestland-managing agencies in the United States will provide our next opportunity to evaluate the influence of cultural values on the forestry profession.

In 1905 a new agency in the United States Department of Agriculture was established: the U.S. Forest Service. Gifford Pinchot was appointed by President Theodore Roosevelt to be the first chief of the agency that would eventually become the largest forestland management organization in the United States.[77] The formation of the U.S. Forest Service ushered in a new era of "conservation" of our forest resources. It must be emphasized that the management principals and concepts of this new agency were based solidly on European forestry concepts and beliefs. Pinchot's principles of "wise use" and "the greatest good for the greatest number in the long run" were based on the premise of providing forest products on a sustained basis for commercial use by U.S. consumers.[78]

The 1860s brought a challenging theory to forest management labeled "preservation." John Muir was the advocate for this theory and challenged the leading conservationists with his beliefs. "Preservation" pictured humans as temporary visitors to the forests and wilderness, held that development and access should be very limited or forbidden, and posited that there was no place for commercial utilization of forest products. These beliefs conflicted with the dominant Western value system, leaving Muir with few supporters. Muir did attract the attention of a few influential leaders, and when the National Park Service was established in the Department of the Interior, the preservation concepts of Muir provided the foundation for the management philosophies of the National Parks.

The two ideologies of management created a conflict that was to intensify when Gifford Pinchot began pushing his conservation concepts. The conflict came to a head when the Interior Department and the Department of Agriculture challenged each other for the right to manage the Forest Reserve lands. Through Pinchot's influence and friendship with President Theodore Roosevelt, he managed to have the original 40 million acres of Forest Reserve transferred to the Department of Agriculture.[79] But the conflict continued, and in 1910 Pinchot was fired as chief of the Forest Service by President William H. Taft, who supported Secretary Ballenger. Taft disapproved of the way Pinchot handled his disagreements with Interior Secretary Ballinger over preservation principals and his insistence that Ballenger had improperly issued no-bid contracts to commercial companies and received kickbacks.[80]

During the time Pinchot was chief, the agency grew rapidly. New employees were being sought and assigned to remote locations in the western states. Living in these remote locations not only required employees to work together but also to live and socialize together. Wives supported husbands by helping with chores around the compounds while their husbands were away for extended periods. Some people frequently referred to the employees as the "Forest Service Family," a tradition that still continues. Morale was high and employees were known for hard honest work and a healthy lifestyle. Throughout my 70 years of close association with the Forest Service, the agency was known for its high morale, and I often heard the agency referred to as the "Marine Corps" of the government civilian agencies.

The efforts of the Forest Service during the early years focused on forest product utilization and protection of the forests from fire, insects, and disease. In 1920 William B. Greeley was appointed the third chief of the Forest Service. Soon after his appointment Chief Greeley wrote, "The national forests are no longer primeval solitudes remote from the economic life of developing regions, or barely touched by the skirmish line of settlement. To a very large degree the wilderness has been pushed back. Farms have multiplied, roads have been built, frontier hamlets have grown into villages and towns, industries have found a foothold and expanded. Although the forests are still in an early stage of development, their resources are important factors in present prosperity. There is probably no large area of forest land in the world on which the use and conservation of multiple resources have been so thoroughly studied or so completely developed in practice as on the national forests of the United States.....Nothing better illustrates the democracy of the American forest policy or the decentralization in administering national forests than the conscientious effort of the Forest Service to weight the importance of different uses on each unit and to give every use its merited place in a bewildering regimen of administrative detail."[81] The emphasis on resources from the forests was strong and focused. As we expanded the National Forest system by acquiring land in the East that had been damaged by logging and land clearing, the agency began a reclamation effort.

The land-managing responsibilities of the agency involved considerable acreage. In the early 1890s the concern over destructive logging, mining, and ranching triggered the passage of the Land Revision Act of 1891. This act provided the authority for the creation of Forest Reserve lands, which were later transferred to the Department of Agriculture.[82]

The United States has a total land base of 2.3 billion acres; today, almost 700 million acres are classified as forestland. Of this, 424 million acres are privately owned, with individuals owning 59 percent, corporations 27 percent, and 14 percent held by estates, associations, clubs, and Indian tribes. The remaining 276 million acres remain in public ownership.[83] Public forestlands are managed by school districts, county governments, state governments, and several federal agencies. The United States Department of Agriculture, Forest Service, today manages almost 193 million acres of National Forest System lands. The lands managed by the Forest Service have been divided into 155 National Forests throughout the United States.[84] Growth of the National Forest System since 1905 occurred as a result of additional presidential proclamations and acquisitions. Almost all of the eastern National Forest System lands were acquired during the 1920s and 30s.

The establishment of the Forest Service ushered in a new era, moving from the gluttonous mining and harvesting of natural resources to the wise use and conservation of resources with a hint of preservation beginning to sneak in. This hint of preservation was led by Aldo Leopold, a Forest Service employee and avid hunter. His idea was to set aside large tracts of land without any road access. He referred to these areas as wilderness hunting areas. His efforts led to the setting aside of the Gila Wilderness Area in 1924.[85] This effort was the beginning of the concept of wilderness as a resource and established the foundation for the later effort to establish congressionally designated wilderness areas. It must be recognized that preservation is the first hint of a dent in the armor of Western values that have driven our entire history of natural resource utilization. To this day, management principles applied to forestlands remain focused on the belief that anything that prevents us from achieving our needs or desires can be changed, manipulated, forced to adapt, or eliminated. White Western European values have dominated the way we react when we encounter something different, such as values and beliefs, people, and concepts of management for our valuable natural resources. Our Western values provided much of the foundation for the basic principles of the forestry profession in the United States, the basic ideology of the Forest Service, and most other forestland-managing entities.

With the increased emphasis on managing forestland comes the requirement of improved access. Early years in the Forest Service emphasized the need to build miles and miles of trails and roads. Roads were expensive and normally built by the timber companies as they accessed the land for timber harvest. The Forest Service basically traded valuable trees for the cost of road construction. The Forest Service gave the timber-harvesting companies valuable timber products equal to the cost of the construction of the roads they were required to build. Most of the roads managed by the Forest Service were constructed with little, if any, monies from the U.S. treasury. This process allowed the Forest Service to become the agency managing the largest number of miles of roads and trails in the United States. Many preservationists became concerned about the increased access and loss of back country and wilderness values.

The direction of the Forest Service was now well established in advocating "wise use" (i.e., conservation) and "sustained yield" (i.e., the harvesting of no more wood fiber per year than was growing annually). These basic principles were intended to meet current demands and ensure an adequate supply of timber products for future generations. However, when implemented, the management actions frequently changed nature, upset forest community relationships, and warped the natural balance of the environment.

The Great Depression arrived in 1929, and with the need for significant employment opportunities, the Civilian Conservation Corps (CCC) was formed in 1933. The program was designed to help relieve the massive unemployment of young men, which the country was experiencing. At the peak, the program employed 3.5 million young men between the ages of 17 and 25 and provided a labor source to accomplish much-needed conservation work in U.S. Forests[86]: such as road, bridge, and trail construction; tree planting; construction of fire lookout towers, administrative buildings, and recreation sites; and major forest protection efforts. It is estimated that the CCC planted over five billion tree seedlings and constructed several thousand miles of trails and roads. The CCC program was a partnership, with the United States Army running the camps and the conservation work programs being planned and supervised by employees of the Forest Service. This program was considered a huge success and would later be used as the foundation for the 1965

Job Corps Civilian Conservation Center programs. In addition to employing many young men, the CCC added great value to America conservation efforts on our forestlands and greatly expanded the firefighting ability and techniques of the Forest Service.

After the start of World War II, the Civilian Conservation Corps was terminated in 1942; however, the accomplishments of the CCC live on to this day. The forest fire-suppression capabilities developed by the CCC provided the emphasis for the Forest Service to become a world leader in forest wildfire science. The CCC's effort also enhanced a transportation system that would eventually elevate the Forest Service to the agency managing the most extensive transportation system in the United States. Today, the Forest Service manages more than 380 thousand miles of roads.[87] This period of history pushed conservation management to a new exciting level.

World War II brought increased demand for almost all natural resources, and wood products were no exception. Improved access by the CCC provided the opportunity to increase timber harvest levels from the National Forests and to increase access for mining and oil and gas exploration. With the large number of men overseas fighting the war and the tremendous need for war materials, women stepped into the factories to produce the much-needed materials for the war effort.

With the return of the soldiers following the war, employment opportunities were needed, and the Forest Service began to expand its workforce. But it was also time to expand the science of forest management. The Forest Service took on the task of developing better scientific data on forest resources. The first effort was to obtain better data on timber resources by a sampling process to estimate the annual tree growth compared to annual mortality. This was accomplished by systematically combining on-the-ground gross sampling with mapping from aerial photography. The process provided reasonably sound data for a forest as a whole to establish annual harvest levels that could be accomplished on a sustained basis. The data was gross but a significant improvement over previously collected data. Armed with this new information, the Forest Service developed detailed Timber Management Plans for each individual National Forest. Each forest was assigned a "potential yield" target, based on the annual growth minus the annual mortality of all the trees growing on the forest. The potential yield established the upper level of harvest that could occur on a sustained-yield basis. The next step was to adjust the potential yield to an "annual allowable harvest level" based on the species and size classes of trees that were considered marketable. These plans provided the basis for annual budget requests to Congress by the Department of Agriculture to finance annual timber harvest programs. The ability to meet and accomplish these harvest levels became the number one element in evaluating the performance of line officers in the Forest Service. Failure to meet assigned timber targets led to reviews from top leadership and in some cases reassignment of line officers to supporting staff positions. During the 1950s the Forest Service was harvesting 10.5 billion board feet of timber annually from the National Forest System land, which totaled more than 190 million acres. The 1960s and 70s saw harvest levels at 11 to 12 billion board feet annually.

From the 1920s through 1940s the federal government purchased hundreds of thousands of acres of land in the eastern United States. These lands were to be added to the National Forest System and were desperately in need of reforestation. The Civil Conservation Corps made a significant contribution to the reforestation needs. After the war, the Forest Service continued to emphasize reforestation, resulting in the establishment of thousands of acres of single-species tree plantations. The effort was enormous and commendable, but I believe it resulted in serious loss of ecological diversity. The resulting plantations were monocultures, and in my estimation, were virtual biological deserts.[88] To further exacerbate the problems, scientists were experimenting with the introduction of nonindigenous tree species to maximize wood fiber production. If one looks at most of these plantations today, they might appear to be well managed, orderly, and properly maintained. In fact, they are void of diversity and of limited value to most living creatures. The lack of diversity opens up these plantations to potential devastating effects for insect, disease, and fire. History demonstrates that the introduction of nonindigenous species of plants and creatures usually upsets the balance of nature and results in unacceptable consequences. One cannot deny that reforestation of these neglected lands was beneficial and that some increase in wood fiber production did occur. The question is whether a more in-depth understanding of nature can provide techniques to reforest these areas in balance with nature and increased diversity in our environment. Can we continue to manipulate nature, or will we learn to live in balance with nature in the future? With more than 70 years of conservation experience in my family, I believe forestry is still basically a profession of tree farming. The focus remains on harvesting valuable natural resources rather than managing healthy individual forest communities. We must begin to recognize and highlight the valuable contributions our forests provide to our human environment in addition to the commodities they provide for everyday living. Change does not come easily, but change we must. Will we finally recognize our stewardship responsibility and role within the environment, or will we continue to insist on controlling the environment?

Chapter 5:
The Seeds of Change

The previous review of the early history of the establishment of forestry as a profession in the United States and the formation of one of the largest forestland-managing organizations on the North American continent clearly demonstrates the impact Western values and principles have had on both efforts. Our quest for wealth and affluence, greed, has influenced the development of science, engineering, and technology, and forestry certainly has been no exception. To further demonstrate the influence our values and beliefs have on our way of life, including science and engineering, we will observe some of the day-to-day applications of the science of forestry by the United States Department of Agriculture, Forest Service. It is important to recognize that our Western values provided the foundation for the development of scientific knowledge of the forestry profession and are not unique to the Forest Service. In fact, the Forest Service is considered a leader in the application of scientific forest management.

My personal experience as an employee with the Forest Service, plus my father's 35-year career in the same agency, provides the opportunity to evaluate the application of forestry on our remaining forestlands. This review will present numerous situations that occurred within the Forest Service to illustrate the agency's focus on resource management rather than forest community relationships. The purpose is to observe what is actually occurring in the application of scientific forest management and determine what may be needed for future administration.

After graduating from the University of Minnesota in 1960, with a degree in forest management, I accepted a seasonal position with the Forest Service on the Ottawa National Forest in northern Michigan. I was assigned to a timber-marking crew on a Ranger District where I was responsible for helping designate which trees should be cut and determining the volume of wood products within each tree. The first thing that became obvious was the dominant role timber harvest had within the district's program of work. The experience also allowed me to observe numerous locations throughout the proposed sale area, where remnants of decadent-large yellow birch logs had been left by past logging operations. I later learned from my father that these now useless logs had been left following a very large timber sale offered by the Forest Service in the 1940s. This sale included several thousand acres of National Forest System land and entitled the private timber company the right to harvest the yellow birch veneer logs throughout the sale area. Yellow birch veneer logs are unquestionably the highest value wood product grown in Michigan's northern hardwood forests. This project resulted in high grading thousands of acres of valuable hardwood forests and caused considerable waste of large volumes of forest wood products. It certainly created massive wealth for some individuals, provided many jobs, and added to the goal of providing community stability. It is obvious, however, that this project considered few conservation-oriented forestry principles or ecological concepts and had little, if any, consideration for other resource impacts and relationships. Consider just the impact on the surrounding environment of construction of the access roads that were required to remove these products. It was difficult for me to accept that this project was supposed to be based on a sound scientific proposal designed to improve forest conditions. The obvious goal was financial greed. This project became the thorn that festered and resulted in my lifelong concerns and questions about so-called scientific forestry practices and principles.

In August of that year, I received a permanent assignment with the Forest Service, and my wife and I moved to northern Minnesota to a Ranger District on the Superior National Forest. As a young forester and new employee, I had much to learn, but the dominant role timber harvesting played in the Forest Service program of work was again obvious. The majority of my time was spent preparing and laying out proposed timber-harvesting opportunities that would be offered for bid to private commercial companies. Most of my remaining time was spent administering timber sale contracts that had been previously purchased by various private companies. This assignment also added to my knowledge of what were referred to as long-term timber sales. The sale that still stands out was a 25-year timber sale contract that was ongoing and had been adjusted by extending the time frame for completion on several occasions, previously. The concept was to provide stability for the logging industry by offering long-term sales opportunities. This particular sale covered most of the district I was assigned to and entitled the company to harvest all jack pine and spruce stands within the sale boundary. The company also had the option of harvesting any aspen stands they wished. This project is another prime example of how our greedy quest for wealth and affluence drives the business decisions of forest management. These long-term sales clearly demonstrated the early Forest Service focus on forest product removal and economic stability but showed a complete lack of the application of forest ecology principles. My concerns about science and engineering, particularly forestry, intensified. But old practices were about to be challenged by outside interests, and slow social change was about to start. Although the change was very gradual if one was truly observant, the changes were becoming apparent.

The passage of the Multiple Use Act of 1960 triggered the beginning of change in the forestry profession and within the United States Department of Agriculture, Forest Service. Concerns from proponents of the preservation management theory were growing rapidly, and the concept of setting aside large areas as "wilderness" by legislative action was expanding. The Forest Service was also about to embark on a new silvicultural process known as clear-cutting. The idea was to copy naturally occurring disasters such as fire, major wind damage, or devastating disease outbreaks, where all the trees are removed at the same time. The result is a single-age and usually a single-species stand of trees with the goal of increasing wood fiber production per acre. Clear-cutting was very similar to a farmer growing corn or other row crops; plant, harvest, and plant again. True, the cycle is over a much longer time frame but the concept is very similar. The other change that was occurring within the Forest Service was the recognition of the need for other natural resource specialists. Range conservationists, wildlife biologists, soil scientists, hydrologists, and other resource specialists were being hired to expand the forest resource knowledge base needed to implement the new multiple-use concepts. The expanded recognition of other renewable natural resources from the forests was viewed as a positive step by many but was somewhat threatening to the large timber companies that depended on the flow of wood products from the National Forest System Lands. Forest management was about to enter a period of slow change.

The new emphasis on multiple-resource staff specialization was a recognition that more than one resource existed or could be produced on a given acre of forestland. In addition to several trees, wildlife species lived and fed on the acre, humans might experience a recreational visit, and livestock might graze on the acre. And so the 1960s brought a new concept to forest management: multiple use. Unfortunately, the new staff specialists tended to serve as advocates only for their individual resource areas, but in most cases they failed to form a resource group capable of identifying and understanding resource relationships. Frequently, resource management conflicts were intensified rather than resolved. Much of the frustration was a result of the dominance of the timber resource.

In 1962 I transferred to an assistant district ranger position on the Mark Twain National Forest in southern Missouri. The assignment was unique in that my district ranger was approaching retirement and experiencing some personal problems. This left me with the responsibility of drafting and implementing the required Ranger District Multiple Use plan. In addition, I found myself faced with an unfinished workload where the pressure to meet timber targets had resulted in the district taking unacceptable shortcuts. Several sales offered in previous years had been only partially prepared. This meant that in addition to the current year's work program, we had to go back and complete work that had been left undone. With the help of an outstanding crew, we managed to catch up and move our emphasis to the Multiple Use Plan. This experience triggered a major concern for me about how to set up a database that would allow for better planning and selection of projects that focused on the health of forest communities. I concluded that we could resolve my concerns by preparing a Multiple Use Plan that recognized forest communities and provided data for each individual community. With the help of a professional forester and the forest soils scientist, we set out to map and sample each community on a 200,000-acre Ranger District. First, a detailed vegetation map of the entire unit was prepared, followed by an equally detailed soils map. It was obvious when comparing the two maps that the soil types were a significant factor in the surface vegetative changes. The similarity of the two maps was unbelievable! The next step was to field examine each forest community and record the needed data. Computers were not in common use at this time, so the use of Mcbee Key-Sort cards was determined to be the best alternative for storing and retrieving data. The database proved to be invaluable in developing sound forestland management decisions for several resources. The State of Missouri, Department of Natural Resources turkey biologists became very interested in the project and convinced me to present a paper on the project at the Mid-West Wildlife Conference at Purdue University in 1964. The State of Missouri covered the expenses involved in the presentation because the Forest Service showed little interest in the project. The paper reported on the use of the data to evaluate wild turkey population carrying capacity. Thirty years later, no one had picked up on this project, and no changes had been adopted by the Forest Service. No one had the insight to recognize the importance of using a detailed database like this to analyze the environmental relationships within individual forest communities and to identify positive and negative trade-offs. Broad-scale, macro-management techniques were, and are, still in place. The forest managers I communicated with expressed concern that the job would be overwhelming because of the thousands of acres involved. Within a two and a half-year period, we were able to finish our mapping effort and complete the initial visits to each community. Those of us who worked on the project saw it as a cyclic effort every 10–15 years, in which each community would be revisited and data would be refined and updated. Certainly, what had been accomplished could and would be improved, but with a strong desire to practice scientific forestland management and a can-do attitude, we demonstrated what could be accomplished. The question is one of what the priorities of the Forest Service should be. Do we focus on how much timber can we harvest, the construction of campgrounds and other resource outputs, or is the goal to improve the health and vigor of our remaining forests, with the forest products being the by-product of our management efforts?

As I indicated, the project became the basis for the completion of the Ranger District Multiple Use Plan. Nationwide, a similar Multiple Use Plan was to be completed for each of the 650 individual ranger districts within the Forest Service, with each unit managed by a district ranger. The planning effort required special multiple-use maps to be completed for each district, but to my knowledge, no other district completed a similar field inventory of each identified stand or community. In my opinion, this one district's effort was the first significant undertaking by professional foresters to attempt to recognize the combination of resources on each acre of forestland. Not only did trees grow on a given acre but numerous species of wildlife and birds lived and fed there, water flowed from the acre, humans recreated, livestock grazed, and oil and gas leasing or mining might occur. The one acre was a complex unit of land. This was a significant change in the evolution of thinking related to the management of forestlands, and it should have pushed the management of forestlands in a desirable direction.

A significant change for my career came in 1965. I was offered an opportunity to temporarily leave the forestry profession to participate in a new government program. Job Corps was an effort to provide work and educational opportunities to young men and women to assist them in pulling themselves out of poverty. It was similar to the Civilian Conservation Corps of the 1930s. This assignment opened my eyes and mind to the importance of human resources. The program involved teaching work skills and work ethics to young men between the age of 16 and 21 who participated in conservation projects on the National Forest System Lands. In addition, enrollees spent half of their time in much-needed educational programs. Many questioned the cost and effectiveness of the program. I will never forget a young man from North Carolina who graduated from the program and wanted to work in a Job Corps center. We managed to place him in a beginning labor position at a Department of Interior Job Corps center. Thirty years later, I learned he had worked his way into the security division of the Park Service and achieved a leadership position in Washington, DC, supervising 50 other security employees. I recognize this is only one success story, but I was privileged to observe many other similar successes. The opportunity to observe and study human desires and needs proved invaluable to me in the remainder of my career. Never again could I focus on the management of natural resources without first considering the potential impacts on human needs and concerns.

As significant as Multiple Use Planning was, the Forest Service still held on to the traditional individual resource plans on each National Forest, which provided the data for the preparation of the annual budget requests to Congress, and timber harvest outputs remained the dominant consideration. Harvest levels throughout the 1960s remained between 10 and 12 billion board feet annually. With increased resource staff specialization, each National Forest began developing wildlife plans, recreation plans, grazing allotment plans, and so forth. As with the timber management plan, none of these resource plans made any adjustments for the impact proposed actions would have on other resource values. Each plan attempted to optimize outputs or production of the individual resource involved without considering the impacts on other resourses and activities.

The 1960s also brought increased attention and interest from environmentalists and preservationists. Groups like the Sierra Club, Wilderness Society, Earth First, and many other groups and individuals began major efforts to institute significant changes in the management of forestlands. Almost all of these groups and individuals followed the earlier teachings of John Miur. Preservation, the removal of humans and their influence from the forests, was often the mission. This drive was triggered by concern over the strong influence of the timber industry on the management of our remaining forestlands. The influence of these groups led to passage of the Wilderness Act of 1964, which formalized the concept of wilderness as a resource provided by our forestlands. The increased interest in protectionism also brought about the National Environmental Policy Act of 1970, which created a large workload for all forestland-managing organizations by requiring them to identify, analyze, and disclose environmental impacts of most proposed management actions. Literally, thousands of person-hours were required to prepare these environmental documents! The result was a significant reduction in time available for scientific on-the-ground management because the increased paperwork came with no additional staff or any adjustments in the required output targets. With limited field time available, these documents were expected to present detailed analyses of environmental impacts based on very little site-specific data and virtually no understanding of forest community relationships. Although these documents identified meaningful environmental consequences, my questions remained focused on the inadequacy of existing data for proper analysis. In our efforts to become more environmentally sensitive to our surroundings, we were removing the professional scientists from the most important responsibility in management of our forestlands. Instead of spending the majority of their time observing and preparing management prescriptions for our forest communities, the job they were educated for and which no one else was prepared to do, they were being forced to dedicate most of their time to preparing reports and justification documents. The application of forestland management was slipping backwards, a trend that has not been reversed to this day.

At this time, national economic interests brought new emphasis on maximizing timber growth on the National Forest System lands, an emphasis that created one of the most intense conflicts in Forest Service history. The research branch of the Forest Service came forth with a proposal to move the silvicultural tool of "Clear-Cutting" to the forefront, because it would maximize wood fiber production per acre. Against the advice of several professional foresters and scientists, the agency took the recommendations for change and fully implemented the clear-cutting proposal for all timber types. I specifically recall Carl Arbogast, a renowned northern hardwoods scientist from Michigan, objecting strenuously to the proposed change but to no avail. He did not object to all clear-cutting but to its use in the shade-tolerant, northern hardwood types. This change demonstrated that timber harvesting was obviously the primary goal, not a tool used to manage various vegetation conditions. Clear-cutting was to become the rule rather than one of several tools available to forest managers. This one change would result in numerous battles and eventually to major congressional action to restrict Forest Service management options in the future.

Clear-cutting is simply one silvicultural tool that attempts to copy the way nature regenerates a stand of trees. It is designed to copy the effects of a fire, major wind event, or a significant insect or disease infestation. It is hard to believe that professional foresters would be trained to apply a variety of silvicultural tools depending on the objectives for the proposed treatment and then for a forestland-managing organization to use only a single harvesting technique. It would be like training a master airplane mechanic and then directing him to repair an engine using only a hammer.

The first step in selecting the proper tool for forest management should be to establish clear objectives that will improve the health and vigor of a given stand of trees or forest community. My professional forestry principles required me to continuously ask why a particular stand had been selected and why a particular treatment had been recommended? The only rationale ever offered was the need to meet assigned timber targets. It is disappointing that after more than 100 years, professional foresters are still driven by assigned targets rather than scientific forestland management objectives. Timber harvesting must be seen as a tool, just like fire or various other noncommercial techniques. Sound forest management decision making demands clearly defined goals and objectives before the professional manager selects or recommends a treatment. Only after establishing well-defined objectives can one select the proper tool. For example, if the only objective is to maximize wood fiber production per acre, particularly in the pioneer tree species, then clear-cutting is the best tool and may be the most cost-efficient method.

The clear-cutting debate became so intense that it eventually led to Congressional involvement. The "Bitterroot Conflict" in Montana symbolized the battle between the Forest Service and the preservation organizations over timber harvesting on National Forest System lands. This conflict involved a debate between the Wilderness Society and the Lolo National Forest over timber-harvesting levels, clear-cutting, and the impact of required access road construction. Arnold Bollie, the Dean of Forestry at the University of Montana, provided much of the leadership for the Wilderness Society. The forest supervisor of the Lolo National Forest, Orville Daniels, and the Northern Region of the Forest Service became a focal point for national debates concerning over harvesting, clear-cutting, and what many thought was excessive road construction. Although German forestry had long been looked upon as a model of sound forest management principles, Bollie referred to Forest Service timber-harvesting techniques in the Bitterroot Valley of Montana as "Nazi" forestry, which suggests a completely different interpretation. This simple metaphor implies a very negative concept of forest management. In West Virginia the clear-cutting conflict focused on the Monongahela National Forest and became the final straw that initiated congressional action. The U.S. Senate decided congressional action was required and set about drafting legislation to resolve the clear-cutting issue. This effort was led by Senators Hubert Humphrey of Minnesota and Jennings Randolph of West Virginia. Fear of prescriptive legislation led Chief of the Forest Service, Max Peterson, to become involved actively with the senators in this legislative effort. The result was the Forest and Rangeland Renewable Resources Planning Act of 1974. This legislation was later amended and expanded by the National Forest Management Act of 1976 (NFMA). If it had not been for the leadership of the Forest Service officials, particularly Chief Peterson, this legislation would have been very prescriptive and would have required congressionally defined exact management treatments to be used. The two senators saw the problem of prescriptive legislation and drafted a bill that expanded the multi-resource management efforts on public forestland but still relied on professional foresters to determine best management practices. The 1976 legislation expanded the Act of 1974 by requiring each region of the Forest Service and each National Forest to develop a Forest Management Plan. Congressman Douglas Bereuter of Nebraska, the only legislator with a background in planning, played a key role in drafting the planning requirements of NFMA. Congressman Bereuter worked as an urban planner with the United States Department of Housing and Urban Development and was the Director of Nebraska's Office of Planning and Programming.

Another evolutionary change that impacted the Forest Service was the election in 1980 of Ronald Reagan as president of the United States. His administration campaigned and was elected to office on the promise of financial conservatism. John B. Crowell, previously an attorney for a large timber company (Louisiana-Pacific), was appointed as assistant secretary of the Department of Agriculture. His leadership and effort to support the administration's conservative position resulted in significant adjustments to the Forest Service's budget requests to Congress. After reviewing the agency's individual resource plans, the administration decided fiscal conservatism would be accomplished by financially emphasizing those resources that produced revenue for the treasury and minimizing financial requests for those resource areas that did not produce revenue. The result was increased budget requests for timber, grazing, mining, and mineral leasing while requesting reductions in the recreation, wildlife, and wilderness programs. In addition to budget adjustments, the review of the timber management plans revealed they could double the timber harvest targets and still maintain a sustained-yield balance on the National Forest System lands. This assumption was true only if one accepted the potential yield calculations and ignored the fact that almost half of the wood fiber identified in the potential yield database was of no commercial value. If the administration had successfully implemented this program, serious overharvesting would have resulted. The grazing resource also highlighted serious questions over the economics of the program administered by the Forest

Service. Western ranchers had held grazing permits for generations on thousands of acres of allotments on public lands and considered these permits to be their grazing rights. Legally, the permits conveyed no rights, only grazing privilege. The average fee for grazing one animal for one month was $1.75, which most non-ranchers saw as a government subsidy resulting in a cost to the taxpayer rather than revenue to the U.S. treasury. The fees were so low that the cost of administrating the program exceeded the return. The concepts put forth by the administration for the management of natural resource programs was about to spark a major debate over the definition of fiscal conservatism. The "Below-Cost Timber Sale" issue was ready to surface.

The below-cost sale issue was the result of the Reagan administration's efforts to emphasize management projects in resource areas that produced revenue and to "de-emphasize" resource projects that did not. However, many special interest groups became deeply concerned and challenged the Forest Service. These interests noted that just because a particular resource produced revenue did not mean it was cost effective. In other words, they argued that if the total cost to complete and reestablish a proposed stand of trees exceeds what can be generated in revenues, then the project is below cost and a timber sale should not occur. Chief of the Forest Service, Max Peterson, insisted that many other resource benefits resulted from the timber sales which provided additional economic benefits. This argument led to an intense discussion of these tangential benefits, such as what a recreation visitor day is worth, what a particular wildlife critter is worth, and even how much a job created by the project is worth. The discussion became so intense that other politicians tried to help resolve the issue. Led by the Montana delegation, members of the House Appropriations Committee directed the Forest Service to provide data to the Congress to support its claims about these various economic benefits resulting from timber-harvesting projects.

In response to congressional pressure, the Forest Service designed a reporting system called the "Timber Sale Program Information Reporting System" (TSPIRS). When the House Appropriations

Committee reviewed the subsequent report, they found it confusing and totally unacceptable. The report failed to provide an easily understood rationale for the various other economic benefits from the large number of Forest Service timber-harvesting projects that cost the taxpayers more to implement than could be recovered in revenues from the sale of the timber. The agency was sent away and told to provide a simple method of evaluating the actual resource benefits and values. Rather than providing an easily understood breakdown of financial costs and benefits, the Forest Service made some minor adjustments to its elaborate reporting system and went back to the committee. The politicians literally threw up their hands, and the Forest Service proceeded to implement a reporting system that would prove, in my estimation, to be a major mistake. The new system simply intensified the debate over how much an elk was worth or what the value was of a single recreational visit, and so forth. What started as an attempt to make the Forest Service more fiscally conservative led to a reporting system that required thousands of employee-hours to routinely prepare but which led to little, if any, benefit. The new reporting system did not save money but adversely affected employee time available for scientific forest management.

At the time, I was serving as the Regional Director for Information in the Northern Region, located in Missoula, Montana. My responsibilities included assisting the Region with problem resolution. I recommended to Regional Forester Tom Coston that we steer the discussion away from economic values and focus on management objectives. We prepared a memorandum directing each National Forest in the Northern Region to discontinue below-cost sales when the only objective was to produce wood fiber. If, on the other hand, clear forest management objectives to maintain or improve the health and vigor of individual forest communities were established with the public, a below-cost timber sale might be the best tool and the most cost-efficient way to accomplish these objectives. In other words, the discussion focused on the rationale for the proposed management action, and the timber sale, the tool, simply became the best method of accomplishing the proposed action. Most public interest groups were willing to accept this concept and were willing to work with the region on implementation. The reaction from the various interest groups indicated that if the Forest Service had, from the outset, focused on discussing and prioritizing sound forest management objectives rather than economic values, the issue of below-cost sales might never have surfaced. This example of the Forest Service response to a request from Congress demonstrates how a bureaucracy can create inefficiencies by increasing the need for reports and documentation; in this case, that inefficiency also intensified the debate over the type and scope of management of National Forest System lands. It also demonstrates that timber harvesting was, at the time, viewed as an objective rather than a tool for the management of forest communities.

While the below-cost sales issue was being debated nationally, the individual National Forests were busy implementing the directives of the National Forest Management Act of 1976. For the first time, the Forest Service was required to develop plans that analyzed all the forest resources together rather than as individual resources. This planning process necessitated viewing all resources at one time, making it difficult, if not impossible, to maximize a single resource. The process forced planners to identify the trade-offs and relationships that would result or change under various forest management proposals and determine which were acceptable and unacceptable. Many Forest Service leaders, including then Chief Dale Robertson, failed to recognize the potential impacts of this integrated planning process, and a few years later when the first plans were approaching completion, they found the reduced timber harvest outputs unacceptable. The timber industry and the oil and gas industry had been actively involved in monitoring the planning process and threatened major legal action if timber harvest levels dropped too low or if significant acres of forest land became unavailable for mineral leasing. The timber industry did challenge the Forest Service's plan for the Bridger-Teton National Forest, claiming projected timber harvest levels were too low to sustain Louisiana-Pacific's sawmill in Dubois, Wyoming. Louisiana- Pacific led the legal action and claimed the reduced harvest levels would necessitate closure of the local mill. This legal challenge turned out to be the focal point for the timber industry's national effort to challenge the Forest Service's planning process. Led by attorneys representing Louisiana-Pacific, a lawsuit was filed in Wyoming Federal District Court against the Secretary of Agriculture, Chief of the Forest Service, Regional Forester of Intermountain Region, and the Forest Supervisor of the Bridger-Teton National Forest, which at the time was me. I received a memorandum, as did the other defendants, from the U.S. Department of Justice indicating they would provide legal counsel; however, I was also told that I could be sued as an individual and might also wish to secure private legal counsel. I also learned quickly that being the last defendant listed on the lawsuit was an extremely lonesome position. If it had not been for my immediate supervisor, Regional Forester Stan Tixier, I would not have received any advice or assistance from the Forest Service. The staff of the Secretary of Agriculture and of the Chief of the Forest Service chose to remain remarkably invisible throughout the court proceedings. The Office of General Counsel in the Department of Agriculture did take an interest in the case, and after the government won the case, they requested I meet with the judge and suggest he publish the case. I did and it was. The Department of Justice provided two very competent attorneys, and the case started with me as the primary and only witness for the government. Careful analysis of Louisiana-Pacific financial records disclosed long-established plans to close the small mill in Wyoming because of its marginal profitability.

Throughout the lawsuit, the strong cultural values of the Forest Service were highly visible. This was a major high-profile lawsuit involving not only the Forest Service but also leadership from the Reagan administration, yet there was no advice or even communication from the administration or the Office of the Chief of the Forest Service. Support from Regional Forester Stan Tixier provided data and assistance needed to prepare me for my court appearance. In addition, staff support was provided by the Regional Office for data collection; however, some professional foresters and one civil engineer within the Forest Service openly supported the position of the timber industry, which was actually interfering with the presentation of the government's position. It became necessary to have them removed from working on the legal case. Because of the few employees who supported the industry's position and wanted the industry to win the case, it was difficult for me to obtain objective data for the legal proceedings. I even received emails from some indicating their objection to information I was presenting and the position I was presenting about the adequacy and accuracy of the Bridger- Teton forest plan. The one engineer became very vindictive toward the forest as long as I was supervisor. As the only Forest Service witness, I presented the Forest Planning process to the court and probably could have influenced the outcome if top management had been willing to communicate their recommendations or desires. The Court found in favor of the Bridger-Teton National Forest, ruling the Forest had properly conducted the planning process and upheld the plan that recommended a much more environmentally sensitive approach to managing the forest. Timber harvesting was recognized as a tool to maintain forest community health and diversity, resource program levels and outputs were accepted as developed in the planning process, the plan provided a realistic strategy focusing on forest health improved biodiversity and a balanced natural environment. The Court determined the plan provided a realistic [...] natural environment, and provided a realistic management strategy focusing on forest health, improved bio-diversity, and a balance of the natural environment.

Concern over reduced timber harvesting on the National Forests, as a result of the forest plans, by the Forest Service's top management was still a major concern and resulted in forced adjustments in several forest plans to minimize adverse impacts on industry and dependent communities. In an effort to enforce old agency cultural and economic values, the Chief of the Forest Service called a special meeting in 1989 in Tucson, Arizona, of all Regional Foresters and Forest Supervisors. The intent of the meeting was to pull everyone together and to direct the Forest Planning process to focus on timber outputs and dependent community needs and stability. Forest Supervisors made a major effort to help the upper-level Forest Service bureaucrats by explaining how the planning process necessitated consideration of trade-offs between the various forest resources, thus making old levels of timber harvesting unsustainable. Everyone was frustrated. Forest and regional personnel offered a sincere effort to help the Chief by reaching out to help the public understand potential impacts. The meeting agenda had been set, and there appeared to be no turning back. A short time after the meeting, Chief Robertson indicated that, after careful review, he felt several forest supervisors needed to be replaced for the good of the agency. In fact, one regional forester and several forest supervisors were offered early retirement options or reassignments to non-decision-making positions. The irony of the situation is that later, at the request of the Clinton administration, Chief of the Forest Service Dale Robertson and Associate Chief George Leonard were given directed reassignments and chose to retire, apparently as a result of their strong support for the timber industry. The below-cost sale issue had taken a significant toll on the leading forest management organization in the United States!

If the national leaders of the Forest Service had been astute to the requirements of the planning process, they would have recognized that we were beginning to observe, analyze, and understand forest community relationships. For the first time, local decision makers were being forced to recognize that for every action there is a reaction. Forest supervisors found themselves in a position of having to decide what trade-offs were acceptable and which were unacceptable. I believe the planning process was indicating an opportunity for a new approach to forest management.

The supporters of change were hard at work within the forestry profession and the Forest Service. During this same period, the preservation organizations were concerned over increased access to public lands. They used the opportunity to get Congress to set aside more wilderness acres. The congressional designation of these areas under the "Wilderness Act of 1964" set them aside in perpetuity, eliminated all motorized access, timber harvest, oil and gas exploration, and most other intrusive management activities.

Today, the Forest Service alone manages more than 35 million acres of congressionally designated wilderness. In my opinion, the involvement of Congress in the process of recognizing legally designate wilderness areas demonstrates a major lack of trust in the government's professional forestland managers by many influential special interest groups. This lack of trust, on the part of many environmental interests, I believe, stems from the strong influence of Western values that are the foundation of professional forestry. If one accepts that wilderness is a natural resource of the forest, then, it should follow that professional forestland management can provide prescriptions to provide and protect wilderness values on certain forested acres. In other words, wilderness should be given the same consideration as other forest natural resources. Public forest managers must realize they are public servants responsible for meeting the management objectives of their employer, the public.

In addition to the many forestry issues of the day, the Forest Service also found itself involved in the nation's social issue of equal employment opportunities for all. A lawsuit was brought against the Forest Service by some of its female employees in California. The courts found that the Forest Service needed to change from the previous European, white, male-dominated organization and culture to an organization that better represented a cross section of the American citizenry. The agency initiated actions to comply with the directions of the courts and employed many additional women and minorities within the organization. Unfortunately, the traditional cultural values of our patriarchal European heritage also influenced how these new employees were assimilated into the agency. The expectation was that they should adopt the traditional founding values of the Forest Service rather than bring in new values that might improve the ability of the agency to offer expanded service to the American public. Nonetheless, the agency began placing some of these new employees in supervisory positions, which were known in the Forest Service as "Line Officers"; however, many of the newly appointed line officers lacked the traditional experience past employees were expected to achieve. The rapid advancement of these new unit supervisors raised concerns among upper-level management. Did the newly appointed unit managers have sufficient experience to make local decisions to resolve local issues? The tendency was to push decision making farther up the organization, making it more difficult for local supervisors to resolve their day-to-day needs and concerns. Even the responsibility for the congressional liaison with elected officials within the state the forest was located, which had always been an important job at the Forest level before, was elevated to the National level.

Probably the greatest gift Gifford Pinchot and the early leaders of the Forest Service left the agency was the strong line-staff organization concept. This organizational structure maximized customer satisfaction by allowing local and quick resolution of public issues and needs. Quality management through customer satisfaction was the cornerstone of the organization. I believe this organizational concept, more than any other factor, is what vaulted the Forest Service into the leadership position for forest management. The implementation of equal employment opportunity left the Forest Service with the dilemma of placing these new employees in line positions with a lack of traditional experience that had previously been required. Upper management's lack of trust in these newly appointed unit managers, line officers, contributed significantly to pushing the decision-making process farther up the organizational ladder, making it more removed from the customers being served. Customer satisfaction and employee morale were beginning to decline.

A new presidential administration, under the leadership of President Bill Clinton, made significant changes to the agency by directing the Forest Service to centralize many services, such as business management, contracting, personnel, and engineering. These organizational changes resulted in further lowering customer satisfaction and employee morale. No longer could business be conducted in local communities in a cost-efficient manner. Centralized specialization was being implemented in the name of progress. I have always believed in the reverse concept, which I call, "de-centralized specialization." My contention is that all employees, in an effort to perform their jobs well, do two things: accomplish work and create work for the next level down in the organization. For example, if you need data and information to accomplish your job, then you create reports and requests for data, which creates work for someone, already busy, at the next lower level of the organization. If you station staff specialists as close to the job site as possible, I believe you will increase effectiveness and efficiency.

Certainly, the 1960s through the 1990s was a significant period of change within the Forest Service. We even reached a point where some resource managers were beginning to talk about ecology and ecosystems. Although I believe the agency lost some of the leadership influence in professional forest management during this time, much of the change did move the Forest Service forward, preparing them for the challenging future. Close observation and analysis of this period highlighted the influence of Western cultural values on the profession and the agency, while wise utilization remained the dominant theory behind professional forest management. Major environmental issues were indicating a need for cultural change, but little change was occurring. Traditional values were still dominating the agency. I still remember Chief Max Peterson repeating time and again during his leadership as Chief of the Forest Service, "We need to find new ways of doing business but hold tight to our traditional values."

Looking back, what were the lessons I learned? What will the future require? Will multi-cultural values finally bring about meaningful change to the forestry profession and society? Will we begin to view our forestlands and renewable natural resources as an intricate part of Mother Earth, the sustenance of life? Will we finally recognize the significant values of our remaining forests to our human environmental requirements? Will Nature's Way, observation and management of relationships, lead us to the desired future? Can we envision a better future, an environment where we are living in balance with our surroundings?

Chapter 6:
Looking to the Future

What does the future hold and what can we expect if we continue to follow our current path? To make reasonably accurate projections requires us to review the facts surrounding our history, past actions, and demands.

The indigenous people of the North American continent saw the bountiful natural resources of our planet as a gift from the "Great Creator". They understood that the sustenance of life came from the natural world and called it "Mother Earth". They have recognized the necessity of living in balance with their natural surroundings, and realized failing to do so could result in bad things happening to their survival.

The Anishinaabe people once lived on the edge of the Great Salt Sea to the East, Atlantic Ocean, in the northeastern US and southeastern Canada. These people today are known as the Ojibwa, Chippewa, Ottawa, and Potawatomi Tribes. According to members of this nation, seven prophets appeared to the people many centuries ago, perhaps thousands of years ago, and foretold the future. These prophecies, known as "The Seven Fires Prophecies of the Anishinaabe", are amazing and offer great insight that can help us understand what is happening to our planet and aid us in predicting our future.

The first six prophecies foretold of the coming of the Light Skinned race from the East and what the people were to do to avoid conflict and to find their chosen lands. The people believe the first six prophecies have been fulfilled and we are living in the time of the Seventh prophecy. The Seventh Prophet was said to be different from the others, he was young and had a strange light in his eyes. He foretold that the time would come when the waters of the earth will become so poisoned that the plants and animals will take sick and begin to die. The prairies and the forests will no longer provide the air needed for life.

When this time arrives, a new people will emerge to find the treasures left along the trail and they will ask the elders for help. The task of the new people will not be easy. At this time, the Light Skinned race will be given a choice between two paths. If they choose the right path, the path of spirituality and balance, the Eighth and final Fire will be lighted, and we will join in brotherhood and sisterhood to prolong life on our planet. If they choose the wrong path, the path of materialism, much harm and even death will come to all the people of the earth.

The wisdom of our indigenous people, amazingly and accurately, provides insight we must become aware if we truly care about the future of humans on earth. It will require the assistance of all people, regardless of where their ancestors came from, to share in finding solutions that will redeem our responsibility of stewardship of our planet. People of all societies must come together, as equals, and join in brotherhood and sisterhood to help each other learn to live in balance with earth. I have come to believe the Book of Revelations, in the Bible, is foretelling the destruction of our planet due to the greedy demands of the human species. It is my opinion, we have the ability to prolong life if we tear down the barriers that exist between cultures and share knowledge that has been passed on from our ancestors.

I am convinced the two biggest environmental issues facing us today are population expansion and deforestation. These two issues have been two of the major causes of the failure and collapse of past cultures and societies. Dr. Jered Diamond, in his book, "Collapse", presents a detailed look at the failure of the Easter Island people, the Greenland Norse community, and the Aztec culture. History provides several examples of the decline and failure of past societies resulting from serious environmental issues.

It is important we take a close look at the current facts surrounding our worldwide conditions, so we can understand what the future might hold. In October, 2011 our world population crossed the 7 billion mark. Just 5 years later, we now exceed 7.5 billion and continue to grow by about 75 million annually. This information has been supplied by the Census Bureau and tells us our world population will reach 10 billion people within the next 35 years. The problem of population expansion is not just due to the birth rate but, is exacerbated by the fact that we are living longer. The Census Bureau also tells us that the fastest growing age class in the world today, is the over 90 year old people. As our world population expands, we can certainly expect the limited resources of our natural world will be stressed beyond what Earth can provide.

Dr. William Rees, professor at the University of British Columbia, states that each individual living in the United States and Canada, require 20 acres to produce the energy and products required to support our affluent lifestyle today. If you divide the current world land base by today's worldwide population, there is slightly less than 4 acres available per person. Our current demands are more than five times greater than what our share should be. What will the demands of 10 billion people look like in 2050? What must we do to prepare and when will we start? Certainly, we can expect intensive pressure on our forested lands to be cleared of trees in order to make room for crops to feed the masses.

To expect a reduction in the rate of deforestation is unrealistic considering the population expansion rate we are experiencing. Coupled with the loss of forested acres is the fact that current forest management practices are destroying the biological diversity which existed within our original forest communities. Management treatments are applied to geographical defined areas such as drainages or hill sides, rather than naturally occurring ecosystems or communities.

It is common knowledge that we have already eliminated a little more than half of the forest cover that once was present on our planet. The past 50 years has seen a reduction in the rate of deforestation occurring worldwide however, recent statistics report that worldwide we are deforesting the equivalent acreage of 20 football fields every minute. Assuming this to be reasonably accurate, within 700 years there will be no trees left. I hear forest scientists arguing that this scenario will not happen, as forestry is similar to farming, and we can simply plant more trees to provide for a sustained flow of products from the remaining forests. The problem is the demand for more acres to grow food crops will overshadow the demand for growing trees. Urban sprawl will continue to gobble-up acreage as well.

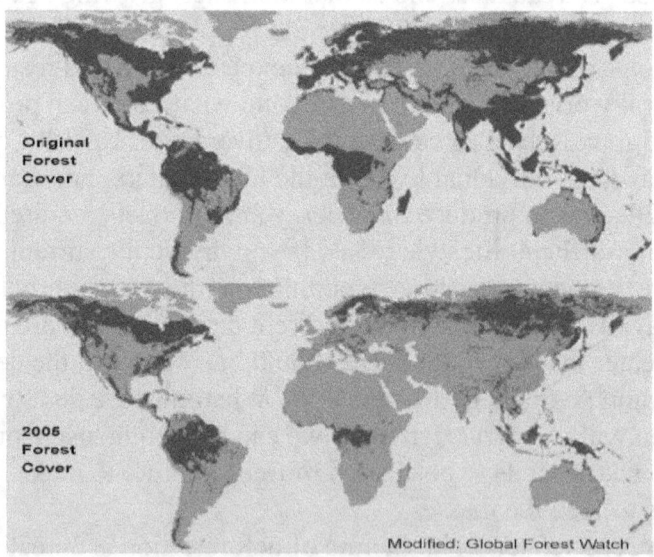

Original forest cover compared to 2005

The other problem is that natural stands of trees are not like a field of corn. They are instead, unique communities based on the physical characteristics of the site they are growing on. The biodiversity and natural relationships that exist within these unique communities are vital to the health of our natural world, and they cannot be duplicated by human agricultural processes. The unique characteristics are the result of the diverse distribution of vegetation, insects, micro-organisms and animal life. Even farmers have come to recognize that a square 160 acre field varies considerably based on physical attributes of each acre. The human division of land has been done to define ownership and to simplify the use of mechanical equipment. A successful farmer must learn to "read the land" and a professional forester requires the same skill.

The alarming fact, which is commonly accepted today by the scientific community, is that at least 70 percent of all living organisms could not survive without forests and, yes, the human species is included. The demise of the Easter Island society was definitely the result of the loss of tree cover due to the near complete removal of trees from their island environment. Our culture seems to believe the availability of natural resources from our remaining forested lands is limitless. The concept of "sustained yield" states: if we cut no more then we grow each year, we will provide an unending supply for the future. This is simply not true! Our forest land base is shrinking every year and our population is continuing to expand, placing an increased burden on the remaining forests.

Our non-renewable resources cannot be replaced. We are told today, by the science world, that today's young adults will experience within their life time, the end of the fossil fuel era. Science will find alternatives, but we are guaranteed major changes in our lifestyle. As land is converted to other uses, the trees will have to go. There are no new lands to discover on our planet where we can plant trees, nor can planting trees create the unique communities of our natural world. I am sure the wealthy hope our space program will discover a new planet which can provide for our needs when this planet fails. Good luck!

A search for a new World

Much of my time has been invested in reading and searching for reliable data that provides the facts about our current environmental problems. The science world strongly supports the findings I have discovered even though there are major disagreements within our political institutions. Many of the opposing view-points are from individuals that state they are not scientists but simply have their own opinions. I am not convinced a scientific education is really required. When I look back at my personal experiences, I believe the significant changes to our natural world as a result of human impacts, are very obvious. Within my lifetime, I have observed the changes in surface water quality with very little surface water left that can be used without significant purification treatment. A large number of our inland lakes now require the use of large quantities of chemicals to control the foreign weed growth so the water can be used just for recreation purposes. I no longer drink from clear mountain streams without filtering the water through ceramic filters.

When I fly over our metropolitan cities on a clear day, I can observe large brownish yellow clouds of pollution covering the cities. Significant changes in weather patterns have occurred. States where major oil extraction is occurring are experiencing unprecedented measurable earthquakes, probably due to fracking.

I had the privilege to interview a person whose family settled in

New Mexico over 300 years ago. He is a student of his family's history and has volumes of photographs and documents to validate the changes that have occurred in the area of their mid 17th century Spanish Land Grant. This area was originally covered with large stands of Ponderosa Pine and waist high prairie grass on the rolling prairie lands. In 1848 this territory was transferred from Mexico to the United States and the harvesting of the forested lands began. By the 1890's, there were five large sawmills operating on 12 hour shifts in the local community. From 1848 to 1930 the timber harvesting resulted in the deforestation of the pine forests. We observed areas once covered with magnificent Ponderosa Pine and tall prairie grass, as he described the changes his family had recorded over the many years they had occupied the land. Today, the area is high-desert with scrubby Pinion Pine and Juniper, the grass is rabbit grass and bunch grass about 6 inches tall, and the once rolling prairie lands are now devoid of top soil which has washed away leaving large arroyos. The shade is gone and the sun bakes the soil to where it is difficult for most of the original plant species to grow. Rainfall today averages 8 inches which mainly occurs during late July and early August. A rancher requires 40 acres to graze one cow for a year under today's conditions. The removal of the forest cover has changed the entire area, including the soil productivity. Those who refuse to accept the climate changes that have been caused by humans, are simply blinded by their greedy selfish demands.

Comparing the changes that have occurred over the past 300 years, according to the family records, provides a sound basis for a detailed look into our future. Empirical observation of the facts allows us to predict with great accuracy what our future expectations for the human species are.

So, what do the historical facts suggest we can expect our future to be like?

First, it is apparent the most significant environmental issue we face is the population expansion.[89] Feeding and caring for over 10 billion people on this planet, will be an overwhelming challenge in just 35 years. There are no new lands to discover on this planet. Birthrates have shrunk slightly in our developed countries but, the elderly are living much longer off-setting any gains. The limited efforts to control population expansion have failed miserably. It is safe to predict that the demand for goods and services will soon exceed the capability of our planet!

We can safely predict the demand for food and shelter will exacerbate the rate of deforestation! The loss of trees will also result in major shortages of pure water, which is the second major environmental issue our world faces. The third critical issue, for us, is the loss of forested lands, deforestation! Life on this planet depends upon large acreages of forest cover. Since we cannot halt deforestation, the health and condition of our remaining forest communities will become critical! Current management strategies for caring for the remaining tree covered lands will fall far short of what will be required. Acceleration of the destruction of biological diversity will continue with the application of current forest science principles, which will amplify the problems of catastrophic wildfires, insect infestations and diseases adversely affecting our remaining forest cover. R.F. Noss in 1990 pointed out that biological diversity is vanishing at an alarming rate due to habitat destruction and over exploitation of the species.[90] It is likely we will experience increased health issues as our population expands and our forested acres continue to shrink. Plants require carbon dioxide for growth and we now know that to produce one pound of wood fiber, a tree absorbs 1.47 pounds of carbon dioxide and releases 1.07 pounds of oxygen into the atmosphere.[91] The importance of trees in sustaining life on Earth is unquestionable!

Recent economic analyses have revealed that the highest-valued natural resource provided by forested lands is clean life-sustaining water.[92]

These predictions are based on an analysis of current facts, but are not new revelations. The Seven Prophecies of the Anishinaabe Nation prove people with an in-depth knowledge of our natural world have been accurately predicting our future for over a thousand years. Some ecologists have been warning of where we are headed for many years. Numerous books have been published, attempting to alert us to the limitations of our planet's resources and the need for adjustments in our life styles. Yet, we sail straight ahead, ignoring the obvious! Maybe, it is because our institutions, corporate, political, academic, and even religious are focused on the individual rather than the stewardship of creation. Is it possible we are such a minute speck in the mystery of life, it is impossible for us to comprehend the magnitude and majesty of creation, and therefore, unable to see and understand what we are doing to Earth. I do not know the reason, but if we truly care about life and future generations, we must be willing to learn to live in balance with our natural surroundings! Remember, what we do to Earth we do to ourselves! We can make a difference and we are capable of influencing the future, but what will be required?

To truly appreciate the importance of changing our demanding appetite for the natural resources of our planet, we must examine our current efforts to mine the earth for the benefit of humans. Even though the United States has major social problems dealing with the distribution of wealth, we still enjoy the most affluent life style of any culture that has occupied a portion of this planet. To support this lifestyle has required us to export large sums of money to purchase resources that are limited or nonexistent on our continent. Fossil fuels are an excellent example. Our thirst for crude oil has resulted in providing the funds to build major military capabilities in several countries that do not share our democratic values. Most of the unrest in the world today is a result of the desire to control the availability of Earth's natural resources, as this provides economic power and control.

As the limitations of Mother Earth become more vivid, many of our leaders and scientists suggest we have nothing to worry about, as advanced technology will provide the solutions needed. It is true we have made unbelievable advancements in science and technology. What was science fiction a few years back, is today reality. Unfortunately, the results of advanced technology has seldom improved the environmental issues we face. Consider the massive advancements that have occurred in the transportation field. One cannot argue that the variety of transportation modes and the accompanying transportation systems has been a very positive contribution to our affluent lifestyle. The environmental impact of the power sources for these different vehicles has actually had a devastating adverse impact on our natural surroundings. It has caused major losses in air quality, losses in water quality, and quantity and even major losses in lands that could provide other human necessities.

Our advancements in the electronics field have provided communications opportunities beyond our imagination. Social networking has made the earth seem much smaller and completely changed our way of doing business. Today, I get my medical test results before my physician has an opportunity to review them. I can bank and shop without leaving my home. I can even run a retail business from my home office. Unbelievable, yet these advancements are not without serious problems. Environmentally, we are now experiencing major problems with the disposal of outdated equipment, much of which is highly toxic to our natural surroundings. I personally find all this advanced technology fascinating, but far beyond my ability to keep up with. All these new smartphones, iPads, computers, blue tooth devices, etc., seem to change every 6 months and most people that are proficient with the equipment, believe they need the very latest updates. In addition to our solid waste disposal problems, this electronic era has had several bad effects on our social structure and there are major problems with cyber hacking and even talk of possible cyber war.

Another vivid example of technological impacts has been the fossil fuel industry. Advancements in technology has allowed us to drill for oil a mile beneath the ocean surface and another mile beneath the floor of the ocean, incredible! When we experienced a disastrous accident and spilled thousands of barrels of crude oil into the ocean environment, we found the technology to finally stop the leak. We should have had the insight to predict such an accident prior to it happening, and designed systems to prevent this catastrophic event. It will take decades to discover the true impacts to the ocean environment. Today, we can force more crude oil from the earth by fracturing the bed rock and then flooding the fractured rock structures. The State of Ohio, in the past five years, has measured over 30 earthquakes, and Oklahoma claims to have measure almost 900 earthquakes in 2015. After being assured it was completely safe, geologists are beginning to suspect these earthquakes may be the result of the hydro-fracking process. Again, with just a little knowledge, we know earth's foundation is a series of plates that are constantly shifting, with your home actually moving 3 1/2 inches west every year. The constant shifting of these plates is evidenced by the volcanic activity and earthquakes we are experiencing on a more frequent basis. The oldest mountains on the North American continent, the Appalachian Mountains, formed when our continent split from the African Continent millions of years ago. It is amazing how just a little knowledge can protect us from future conflicts and problems. Yes, it is unbelievable how science and technology has forged ahead without linking the importance of the human element to the scientific knowledge base and the development phase of resource extraction.

My education and professional experience has focused entirely on the management of public forestlands. I admit there have been significant advancements in the education of specialists in the individual resource areas and with the addition of some ecology education requirements. Even technology has made significant advancements in the field of communications, GPS technology, and aerial photography using drones. Today's planning procedures provide a much better understanding of the inter-connectedness between the various natural resources. Yet, I remain convinced our current management philosophies are far from adequate for the future. Numerous scholars have suggested that it is our cultural values that set the stage for how we interact with one another and view our relations with our natural surroundings. The Western Civilization has long been driven by capitalism and the quest for wealth and fluency. The human demands of the past 300 years have left our planet requiring human help in the form of stewardship and caretaking. Preservation is no longer a viable option!

Back in the late 1850's, John Muir's concept of allowing the natural world to follow the natural cyclic processes of regeneration without the influence of humans, may have been a logical consideration. Much has changed, and current demands of 7.5 billion people on our natural resources requires active management and assistance to assure an acceptable future. The time has long passed for the Preservation theory of management.

In the 1880's, our first forestry scientists instituted a new concept of management which Gifford Pinchot labeled "Conservation", "Wise Use and Sustained Yield". This management philosophy has provided the basis for forestry education and management of public and private forested lands over the past 125 years. Conservation focuses on the management of the individual resources, at the neglect of biological diversity and ecological relationships. I accept that these renewable natural resources have made a major contribution to the development of the most affluent society the planet has ever seen, but I am convinced the principles of "Conservation" will not provide for our future needs.

Our ability to predict the future also requires a review of past leadership in the forestry field. Leadership in both corporate and public forestry organizations are counted on to provide the initiatives for future management policies and directions. It requires visionaries who observe, in detail, our surroundings and social changes, and can then design solutions to help achieve desired future conditions for the citizens. My experience was in the public arena with the United States Department of Agriculture, Forest Service, so this is where my examples come from. I am sure similar examples have occurred in corporate leadership.

The enactment of the National Forest Management Act of 1976, initiated a new era for the Forest Service. This Act required the Agency to implement a new planning process for each National Forest within the Agency, at the time 155 separate units. Forest management, from 1905 to 1976 had focused on managing the renewable natural resources from the forests. Yes, we had all kinds of plans for each resource and had been developing and revising these plans for 70 years. Unfortunately, too many of the Agency's leaders failed to recognize the changes this new process would require. This new process mandated that the manager must identify the relationships between the various resources thereby, making it impossible to maximize the production of any one resource. The past focus on timber harvesting outputs was going to be seriously impacted. The Conservation concepts of maximum timber harvest level to provide for dependent community stability was going to be challenged. At the time, the Forest Service was selling an average annual volume of 11.5 to 12 billion board feet of timber to commercial timber harvesting companies. Yes, these outputs took into account the growth and mortality rates of the trees, "sustained yield", but failed to consider the impacts on other forest resources. As the first Forest Plans began to reach completion, it was obvious we would not be able to continue historic levels of timber production. The reality was, the planning process required each local decision makers to identify and analyze the trade-offs between the different resources and then decide which trade-offs we could live with and which we could not.

Forestry leadership must recognize and accept what the evolution of planning has taught us. "Wise Use" and "human community stability" were honorable goals in the past but, they will not provide the path to our desired future. Observing the multitude of relationships we share and require from our forested lands provides the understanding and appreciation for how we must manage these valuable forests in the future. Goals that focus on what we can take from the forests have driven the science in the past, but must be adjusted for the future.

One cannot expect detailed treatments of the diverse forest communities without site specific knowledge of the lands one is responsible for managing. You simply cannot sit behind a desk and read the land! Today, most professional scientists in public agencies spent 60 percent to 80 percent of their time managing budgets, filing out reports, writing environmental justification documents, and reporting accomplishments. Sadly, much of the information used to prepare the project environmental impact statements is textbook data that does not provide the specificity required for the proposed actions.

The final concern with current management is the fact that the science of forestry was founded on the principles of agricultural farming, and these principles continue to be applied. These farming principles were the basis for the development of the theory behind Gifford Pinchot's "Conservation" management concept and are the reason the Forest Service was placed in the Department of Agriculture. This concept has resulted in the planting of billions of trees in plantations. Seems like an honorable thing to do however, it has resulted in large areas of single species plantations that destroyed bio-diversity. In the 1970's and 80"s, our government passed legislation designed to encourage tree planting by private citizens. This also seems like an honorable effort, but once again, we are destroying forest diversity. I know these trees store carbon dioxide, prevent soil erosion, produce oxygen, and help purify our water, but there is a better way. These monocultures can be biological desserts for other living organisms and are usually far more susceptible to catastrophic attacks from insect and disease infestations and destructive wildfires.

Single species, single age pine plantation

The late 1970's brought many changes to the Forest Service organization and staffing. To begin with, the Multiple-Use and Sustained Yield Act of 1960 influenced the Agency to consider the need for specialized scientific personnel. The Agency began to hire a much broader range of scientists to amplify the new emphasis on multiple-use. The National Forest Management Act of 1976 added more incentives for increased specialization. The planning process required the planning teams to integrate the various natural resources resulting in the identification of the variety of positive and negative impacts between the resource relationships within the individual communities and provided improved scientific knowledge for the management of our National Forests. Specialization should have been a very positive addition to the Agency however, leadership failed to establish an environment that required the team approach to integrate resource management goals and objectives. Instead of a team approach, I experienced the specialists becoming advocates for their specialty which often tended to intensify the debate, rather than find desirable alternative solutions.

The 1980's also brought a significant change in the number of women and minorities to the Forest Service. Directed by the Federal Courts in California, the Agency began building a staff that better represented a cross-section of the American society. Again, this direction should have been an opportunity for adjusting the Agency's values to provide better public service for the American citizens however, this is not what I observed. In an effort to comply with the court, people were promoted to managerial positions with far less experience than previously was required. Leadership promoted these people but, withdrew much of the authority and responsibility for local decision making. The last 25 years has seen a loss of employee morale, mainly due to lack of trust, and has also resulted in serious loss of local community involvement and trust for the Agency. Resolving problems at the local level builds relationships and trust and was one of the most ingenious staff organization concepts instituted in the early years of the Forest Service.

After seeking the facts and observing the history of forests and our natural world, what will the vision of the future be? First, we must accept that there is little we can do to control population expansion, and the predictions of growth are reasonably accurate. The growth patterns will also continue resulting in significant expansion of our urban areas. Our global economy will expand and our ability to control our own economic factors will become more difficult. Science and technology will continue to advance, making for an easier life style worldwide. Many third world countries will develop stronger economies and create increased demand for earth's limited resources. The availability of fossil fuels will be exhausted within the next 60 years and, although we will discover new energy sources, life will change significantly. The demand for human labor will continue to shrink as it is replaced by advancements in technology, robotics, and machinery.

Deforestation will continue at an unacceptable rate, due primarily to increased demands resulting from population expansion. Urbanization will eat up large amounts of land to provide for housing development and recreation area expansion. To feed the growing masses of people, we will need to convert lands once covered with forests, to agricultural uses. Genetic alteration of our plants and animals will result in both positive and negative impacts on our food supply and our environment. Pure water supplies will experience serious shortages and some arid areas may have to be abandoned. Air pollution and toxic waste disposal will intensify and create major health issues. In 700 years our forests and trees will be gone! Do we have to accept this vision or can we find a better future?

Chapter 7:
A Call to Action

Finding a better path to a more desirable future will not be easy and will require the assistance and support from each one of us. The first thing we must do is slow down (think slow) long enough to observe and accept the facts that are obvious if we but read and view what is happening all around us. Nothing will change unless and until we want it to. I am an optimist and truly believe the damage humans have caused to our planet can be repaired and restored if we focus our intellect and work ethically on the environmental issues we face.

Most religious scholars now accept that the story of creation found in the Bible, in the Book of Genesis, contains several words that misinterpret the original Hebrew intent. Today, it is commonly accepted that the proper interpretation of the words "dominion", "domination" and "control", should properly be "stewardship" and "caretaking". Yes, the Bible is actually assigning all of the people on earth a responsibility of caring for the planet and the gift of life! Earth does not belong to us; we are simply one small part of the mystery of life on Earth!

Are we at the fork in the path where we must choose which direction we are to follow to a desired future? Are we actually in the time of the Seventh Prophecy of the Anishinaabe People? What path will we choose; the path of spirituality or the path of materialism?

The "null" or do nothing alternative is obviously unacceptable, so what are our options? In other words, simply following our current direction will not result in a future we can accept! We need to begin searching for alternative solutions that are realistic and allow us to maintain a reasonably affluent lifestyle as we work to understand and support our valuable natural world we depend upon.

There are a few givens which we will have very little ability to change. We have no undiscovered lands left to provide additional opportunities to provide natural resources for our expanding population. The search for information about our Universe and developing technology which will allow improved travel between the various planets will continue, however, I seriously question the rational that drives this quest. The costs involved and the potential of a successful conclusion, raise serious questions over this effort. I am sure these space efforts will continue and, all I can do is to wish them well. So, it looks like we are stuck with what we have, planet earth. To me this suggests that every acre must perform at its optimal potential, which means intensive management of the unique forest communities.

There have been some attempts to control birthrates and population growth, but the success has been dismal. Hopefully, the birthrate will continue to slow as it has since the 1960's, but it is evident we will have to accept the projections for future population growth. Ten billion people by 2050, appears realistic and unavoidable. Once again, the demands for production from every acre will intensify, and proper management appears to be the only option to maintain the health and vitality of the land.

I am sure science and technology will continue to search for ways to manipulate Mother Nature in hopes of forcing her to provide more. The results will produce unacceptable consequences for our planet, but hopefully we will find some new processes that might alleviate some of our environmental problems.

The first step, which I have already suggested, is to define and accept the problem. This will not be easy, as accepting the obvious problems means accepting the need for change. Because of the economic impacts and life changing effects, we are observing a political debate over the causes of environmental issues we face on a daily basis. The wealthy entrepreneurs are constantly, wanting a free hand to do as they like with their business investments. Regulations, designed to protect the employees and the public consumers, are considered unacceptable obstacles that disrupt profits. During the 1920's, corporate America clearly demonstrated they were not willing to care for the employees they depend upon without Labor Unions or Government regulations. Labor Unions have lost their influence and effectiveness and benefits, such as health insurance and retirement programs are disappearing rapidly. The transfer of jobs to overseas locations is actually a planned movement on the part of corporate American to revert to the "good old times" of the 1890's to 1930's, where labor was forced to work in deplorable conditions. A continuation of this movement against labor will force more government responsibility to provide for the welfare of the American population, particularly the elderly.

Is not the vision of our future a clear problem statement that requires our attention? Change must come, and soon! Cultural values are the set of values our social system has developed and incorporated into our daily lives over many generations. Changing any of these values is extremely difficult, and often requires a significant emotional experience for the change to occur.

With a problem statement clearly defined, we need to search for alternatives in several categories. Our call to action must include what we, as concerned citizens, need to do, changes that can improve our educational programs, adjustments needed in our academic curriculums for our scientists, major recognition and supporting actions required of our political representatives, and significant adjustments needed in the management of our public lands, particularly our forested lands.

Our call to action must examine each of our institutions and suggest changes that might allow for a more desirable futuristic outcome. I certainly do not have all of the answers needed to solve our environmental problems, but my limited effort may trigger others to get involved in our quest for ways to improve our future outlook.

If we are to make changes in our society's values and lifestyles, we cannot overlook the importance of education. I would suggest that even though our college science curriculums are now incorporating ecological principles into many of the resource management studies, our citizens continue to have very limited knowledge of the ecological relationships within our natural world. Our early education, our life experiences and our cultural values have focused on how to be successful as individuals. Today's lifestyle emphasizes the importance of money, wealth, and affluence, and what we must do to achieve success. Little, if any, time is devoted to teaching the story of creation and our connection and dependency with the multitude of relationships we share within our natural world. If we cannot see or understand these connections and relationships that are a part of this complex planet, Mother Earth, why would we be concerned about the damage we are doing to the natural world we require for life? Our motto will remain take what we want today and don't worry about tomorrow!

Education is a mandatory starting point for change. Because changing cultural values is so difficult, I am convinced our education efforts must focus on our youngsters in the elementary and intermediate schools. Students in this age group are eager to learn new information and concepts, and are not yet cluttered with the economic and lifestyle concerns adults are blinded by. They are open to new ideas, new opportunities, and new insights. The major problem we have in reaching many of our youth is overcoming the influence from the surroundings in which they are growing up. We are becoming a more urbanized society, and our youth seldom have the opportunity to observe or experience the natural world.

I am reminded of an experience I had in Job Corps back in 1965. We had 160 young men between the ages of 16 and 21 in a rural conservation camp. One night we had a lunar moth hatch and the screens on the dormitory windows were covered with hundreds of moths. Lunar moths are very large, sometimes 6 to 8 inches across their open wings. Most of my young men were from urban environments and had never seen moths like this. They were scared to death and it was a very exciting time until we managed to settle things down by getting everyone together and explaining what was happening, thereby assuring them there was no danger. I can imagine what it must be like to experience one's first trip into the dark forest. Even so, we must find a way to teach our inner city youth about the natural world and how connected to and dependent upon that world they are.

My wife and I believe this to be so important that we have decided to focus our efforts on this opportunity. Environmental education has been incorporated into our public schools over the past 20 years, however my experience in reviewing classes at the high school level has shown that most of the material deals with individual resources such as trees, animals, plants, and natural processes like transpiration or photosynthesis. I found no discussion designed to incorporate the human element into the science, and no ecological discussions that helped the student see the complexity of the relationships that exist in the natural environment.

Our plan is to pursue an effort to adjust the way our teachers present environmental education. Our vision is to develop a series of short videos for use in the public schools. These videos would be designed to provide introductory information to initiate a discussion on individual natural resources. Each program would present the science information and show how the resource is connected to life systems and the human requirements. The plan is to involve college students studying natural resource programs, to develop 8 to 10 minute videos that focus on how humans rely on earth's natural resources for life. The effort would make these videos available to public school teachers, free of charge, over the internet such as you-tube. Once a process is in place to produce a flow of videos on a variety of subjects, we will need to market the concept to our public school teachers. We truly believe this program is more important than any other thing we can do to provide a positive change that can prolong our future.

Helping our youth understand how the human element is connected to science, may seem like a simple idea that can be implemented quite easily, however I can assure you that implementation will require the active support and involvement of each citizen, particularly parents of these young people. Parents must take the time to become aware of the facts that identify these environmental issues. As a parent, you are responsible for helping your children understand how we are connected to the natural world and how our survival depends on the relationships we share with other creatures and organisms. Grandparents, who may well have experienced life growing up close to the land, need to assist their grandchildren experience and appreciate our natural surroundings. We need parents to play an active role in insisting that the schools prepare our youth for the challenges of living on this planet as well as how to find a job and survive economically. Environmental education cannot be thought of as an interesting additive, it must be seen as a mandatory curriculum for all students.

We all need to introduce our youth to the natural world by taking time to visit the outdoors and observe the beauty of our natural surroundings. You can do this in your backyard, in the local park, or, even better, a trip to the countryside. Even the grass can be used as an example to demonstrate how plants add nutrients to the soil, prevent soil erosion, and absorb moisture into the soil. The important thing is to teach your children the relationships we share with other living organisms. The other important factor is to help the young understand there are limits to what earth can provide. It is possible we can run short of clean water or experience insufficient oxygen for our expanding population.

Voters need to contact and insist that their elected officials understand their needs and demands and hold the representatives to solving environmental issues, rather than worrying about acquiring funds to finance their campaigns. We need to insist on term limits on our Congressional members and withhold our vote when they fail to do the work of the people. The government is us, the voters; it is the leadership that is broken. Our vote is a powerful tool that needs to be used wisely to ensure our government leaders fulfill their responsibility to the people. Meaningful change must start from the bottom, which can only happen when you and I come together and insist our elected officials implement solutions that begin to provide for our every day needs. We can make a difference! Yes, there is no substitute for the power of the people when we join hands on common issues. Even though we must organize and insist on revolutionary change for the future, we will require the action of our academic, government, and corporate institutions to make the needed transition. What must we expect from these institutions?

Academic change

Prior to 1900, there were very few opportunities in the United

States, for advanced educational studies in natural resource management programs. This was particularly true in the field of forestry. During the 1800's, German forestry was the example others tried to copy. Individuals in the United States, wishing to get advanced education in forestland management, found the opportunities were either in Germany or France. Soon after 1900, a few schools initiated new curriculums in natural resource management. The 1930's brought the CCC program to provide job opportunities for the large number of unemployed young men. This program introduced thousands of young men from the cities and farms, to the natural world. I believe their experiences gave them a whole new outlook on the importance of our natural surroundings and provided an incentive for them to pursue opportunities in the field of land management. This program demonstrates how peoples' respect for our connection to and dependence upon nature can be changed by introducing them to a different environment. Our youth can and will respond when given the chance to experience the wonders of nature.

Since the early 1900's our colleges and universities have expanded and improved their programs in natural resource management. Advanced technology has provided tools and procedures that can assist the scientist in reading and treating the land. Research has developed new products from wood and ways to increase the production of wood fiber per acre. Improved ecological studies allow us to predict environmental consequences of proposed management actions and current planning processes provide a deeper insight into the multiple relationships found within the natural world. Unfortunately, little has changed regarding how and why we manage our valuable public lands that still exist. Our quest to maximize wood fiber production has placed even-aged-management as the preferred management strategy for many different timber types. Even-aged-management uses clear-cutting as the primary silvicultural tool and all too often is applied to large areas, as shown in this photograph.

Vast clear-cuts covering thousands of acres

My father graduated with a degree in forestry, from Michigan State University in 1936 and spent 35 years in the United States Department of Agriculture, Forest Service. I completed my degree at the University of Minnesota, and immediately received an appointment with the United States Department of Agriculture, Forest Service. Together, we represent 70 years of experience in public forest land management. I feel qualified to point out that major advancements have occurred in academic forestry scientific knowledge, improved technology, scientific specialization, and technically improved planning processes, however little if any changes in the goals for managing our valuable forested lands have been proposed or implemented. The goals of management, since the beginning of forestry science in American academic study, have been to focus on the resources we can take from the forests. There has been a very slow evolution from managing a single resource to multiple-use, which recognizes more than one resource, can be managed on each acre, and now to the National Forest Management Act that requires some realization of the relationships between resources. This is a definite improvement, but if you review employee job descriptions and performance standards, you will see that they focus on meeting assigned targets, producing reports, and living within budget constraints. Never have I seen standards that measure quality of detailed knowledge about the unit of land they are responsible for, or condition of the forest cover health and diversity.

Refocusing our management goal to forest health begins with the education these employees receive at the higher education facilities that offer natural resource programs and continues with the leadership that set these work standards. If we are to experience improved management of our valuable forested lands, it must start with the education process for our future forest land managers.

The first change is to require students wishing to acquire a degree in any natural resource area to complete courses in ecology and have a sound understanding of relationships within our natural world. The student would then move on to specialized course work in the particular resource area of interest. I believe knowledge of relationships is far more important than detailed scientific knowledge on an individual resource element. The ability to observe the unique differences between the various forestland units and the variety of interactions within each unit, defines what I call communities. If the scientist does not see these unique features that identify the individual communities, they will not be able to adequately manage the forest units for health and diversity.

To clarify my use of the word community, let me give an example. I hunt a 35 acre wood lot with two friends. Over the years, I have observed the complexity of this small 35 acre tract and the relationships that are a part of each unique unit within the tract. There are four separate communities within the tract. The northwest corner has a heavy sandy loam soil with a clay hard pan 18 feet beneath the surface, which prevents surface water from percolating into the ground. Shallow puddles are found within the unit most of the summer and there is a man made pond that holds water year-round. The major species of trees are aspen, some green ash and an occasional soft maple and the under story is dense shrubs that are difficult to walk through. The deer and the turkey use the area for hiding, cover, and travel ways. The insect life is dense and so the animals tend to move through, using this area only for escape routes. Just to the east, the elevation raises about 2 to 3 feet and the drainage improves slightly. We begin to pick up more maple trees and a couple of black cherry trees, as well as a few northern white pine trees. An occasional black and fox squirrel can be seen, and although there are a few water puddles, they tend to dry up faster. The underbrush begins to thin out and tree density increases. The primary animal use is for travel ways, to and from feeding areas and water holes. Moving to the south, the elevation raises rapidly by about 15 to 18 feet. This area has well-drained sandy loam soils and a deep layer of organic top soil. The tree species changes dramatically to red oak, hard maple, northern white pine, and an occasional white oak and tree growth also improves with larger diameter and taller trees. Heavy mast crops are common in this area and it is the favorite feeding area for many of the animals that live nearby. The rodent population is very evident, with chipmunks and a variety of mice being prevalent. In the fall there are large areas where the turkeys are scraping the leaves away to locate acorns. It is a busy community, especially in the fall and spring months. There are cultivated fields on three sides of the 35 acres, which supply much of the required food during the summer and fall seasons. To the south is a large wooded unit which is 280 acres in size and is a private hunting preserve and inaccessible to the public. There is obviously dense cover located on this parcel as the deer find thermal cover and hiding cover during the daytime somewhere on the unit. The southwest corner of the 35 acre tract is another unique community that drops down about 12 feet to a well drained sandy site. Almost all of the trees are quaking aspen with a few planted white spruce trees. The spruce trees provide some hiding cover for deer and turkeys, and the aspen provide some browse, but animals primarily use the area for travel routes.

I recognize science today refers to eco-systems but, I prefer the word community, as it is better understood by the public and strongly suggests the mix of relationships that are functioning within the land unit. To maintain or enhance diversity we must maintain the integrity of the community. The description I have just presented provides the basis for a new set of principles for the management of our remaining forested lands, which I call, "Nature's Way". This is the kind of ecological foundation our graduating natural resource scientists need to bring with them to the work place.

The other area of need in training scientists for the field of forest management is people skills. There is a need for managerial leaders in public agencies and private corporations, and the usual way of selecting these people is based upon the employee's performance in the work setting. There is no question that some individuals are better at working with people than others, but our academic institutions are more than capable of improving the people skills of students interested in working toward a career in management. Those of us working in the public sector are referred to as "public servants", and there is a reason for this label. Our responsibility is to serve the public.

One of the most frustrating issues I see daily in the public service arena is the difficulty of implementing solutions to complex problems. We read every day of legal intervention by a variety of environmental and corporate groups supporting or opposing actions of the public agencies. When I review many of these confrontations, it is apparent that the decision maker failed in many ways to work with the potentially affected interests. Most decision makers, when they hit a road block, redouble their efforts in the technical process, failing to realize the problem is on the people side of the process. There are training courses that can prepare students to be effective decision makers.

I am familiar with one course that focuses on preparing people, already in public and corporate positions to be more effective in implementing solutions to major issues and problems. It is called "Citizens Participation by Objective", offered by the "Instituted for Participatory Planning". The course was developed and is taught by Hans and Anna Marie Bleiker, from Monterey, California.[93]

In the 1960's a group of students at the Massachusetts Institute of Technology (MIT), completed their doctorate thesis, which analyzed why the solutions to major complex problems in the public and private sector had such a low success rate for implementation. The conclusion was that the failure rate was primarily due to the inability to achieve "informed consent" with the potentially effected interests, or in other words, inadequate public involvement. One of the students was Hans Bleiker, who, with his wife Anna Marie, went on to develop a consulting company that utilized the findings from the study to provide a course which trains people in management positions how to improve their problem solving skills.

The course of study begins by defining the problem with the involvement of people that will be affected by the recommended solution. The old adage holds true here, "If there is no significant problem, why fix it?" If you cannot define a compelling problem, you need not spend anymore time working on a solution. I cannot over emphasize the importance of this step.

The next requirement is to make a complete list of the potential affected interests. You cannot overlook any group or individual or you may get derailed at the end of your process. Next, you must open communications with each interest personally, and do not assume announcements in your local news media will suffice. You must make an effort to invite each and every person and make sure you keep them up-to-date throughout the entire process.

Once your interests agree there is a problem that needs to be solved, and you are sure you have contacted all of your potentially affected interests, it is time to begin developing a range of alternative solutions. Compare each potential solution to the "null alternative", or the do nothing option. You must be able to define the positive and negative effects of each proposed solution, or it is not a legitimate alternative. It is your responsibility to select the best solution, but you will be expected to present your rational for your selection. Your goal is to reach "informed consent", which means your interests may not fully agree, but they are willing to withhold their veto. On a scale of 1 to 10, informed consent is 5.5.

Self-made managers and leaders are no longer adequate and we must help in their development through our academic institutions. Higher education programs designed to encourage career employees to return for educational opportunities are needed to prepare them for advanced positions within their company or agency. Our country is in desperate need of implementation geniuses.

My final recommendation for our natural resource colleges and universities is to teach the scientist, the importance of having a tool box full of tools specifically designed for the unique conditions that are present in each community. The process of managing each unique unit in the forest is to establish management objectives and then select the proper tool or treatment. When the Forest Service decided to emphasize the concept of even-aged-management with the use of clear-cutting back in the 1960's, I became very concerned and had serious questions accepting that forestry was simply an agricultural process. Yes, trees are plants, however, forests are far more complex and diverse than a field of grain and demand very different management considerations. Forests are a part of our natural world and were created with extremely diverse conditions between the communities that make up the forest. It is time we manage the forests instead of the natural resources we take from the forests!

Our academic institutions have been on the leading edge of advancements in science and technology these past 50 years but, we have failed, throughout our society, to connect the scientific knowledge to the human element. Certainly, our higher education institutions must play a key role in future management directions.

Management Change

The management of our remaining forested lands is where we need aggressive change to be initiated, as soon as possible. Time is not working in our favor as the world population expands and deforestation continues. It is, therefore, crucial that management of these forest environments must function at peak performance levels. To accomplish this goal will require a far more intense effort to keep these valuable forests healthy and vigorous. Resource scientists must be directed to get out from behind their desk and become familiar with the lands they are responsible for. Top management must insist on a much more rigorous collection of data about the forest communities so scientists can prepare professional prescriptions that will improve forest health and diversity. The very first step is for leadership to redefine the management goals for our remaining forested lands to reflect our commitment to forest health and diversity and build this mission into job descriptions and performance standards.

Leadership must make it clear the goals are the forests conditions, and the by-product of proper management will be forest products needed by the public. I remind you this management philosophy is referred to as "Nature's Way".

Supporting this new concept of management should result in changing typical organization staff structures. Since the early days of forestland management, most organizations have structured their staff by individual resources. They had a staff unit for timber, one for wildlife, one for grazing, and so on. The age of specialization added several new resource scientists with each one representing their specific resource. Fitting these specialists into the typical staff structure encouraged each scientist to become an advocate for their particular interest. What was needed was an inter-discipline team approach to identify and analyze relationships that were present and what impacts might result from various management applications. New staff structure ideas are needed that will encourage a team approach to forest planning, with a focus on relationships.

I would suggest the most important need from management is the establishment of clear goals for the management of forest communities. This can be accomplished through mission statements, job descriptions, and performance standards. The mission must focus on the condition of the forest cover and not on resource outputs. We must encourage the field scientists to establish site specific objectives before selecting the proper tool to use, and they need to have the authority to select from a full tool box. An emphasis on even-age-management must be replaced with directions to achieve health and diversity of our remaining forested lands. Coupled with this direction, we must implement a major paperwork reduction effort to allow our field scientists to return to the lands they are assigned to manage. We need our professional scientists developing prescriptions of each community that will maximize the efficiency of each acre of our limited forest covered lands so we can achieve maximum benefits from the contribution these communities make to life on our planet. The by-product of good management will be the valuable goods and services from the forests.

The 1980's brought pressure from the preservation special interest groups to encourage change within the science of forestry. These groups and individuals believe that protection of our natural environment can best be achieved by excluding humans and allowing nature to take her course. Human demands have expanded to the point that our natural world requires management assistance from those who are creating the increased demands. By the early 1990's, the pressure these preservation groups brought did get the attention of a few Forest Service employees who thought they could provide some new management concepts which would improve support from so-called environmental groups. Terms such as eco-systems and ecological concepts became common in discussions on forest management principles. There were some within the Agency that saw this as a new management concept and believed they were instrumental in developing and defining these new principles. When I read and thought about what was happening, it was apparent that these new concepts were actually thousands of years old. Review of American history clearly demonstrates that many of these, so-called, new ideas pertaining to human relationships with nature have existed for millennia. Many scientific scholars have been trying to elevate these environmental issues and concerns for the past 150 years. We do not have to re-invent the wheel, but simply observe and learn from the past. The major question is, why has it taken so long to realize the importance of living in balance with the capabilities of Earth? The answers, I believe, rest squarely on our traditional western cultural values of domination, greed, and conquest. We believe we can manipulate our natural world to produce what we demand, and that is the path we are following today. Chemical fertilizers, genetic alteration, forced even age management, non-indigenous tree plantations, are all examples of our attempt to manipulate nature.

The following list contains recommendations for us to consider as we work to manage forests, wood lots, city parks, and even our back yard:

1. Accept the fact that the real values of our remaining forests are the trees themselves, not the products we can make from the trees.
2. Understand that forestlands are a collection of small individual communities.
3. Intensify our power of observation so we can learn to "read the land".
4. Focus management goals on forest health, vigor, and bio-diversity.
5. Develop databases containing detailed information on individual communities.
6. Initiate management actions that harvest decadent and diseased vegetation while maintaining important natural relationships.
7. Avoid introducing non-indigenous plant and animal species even when it might increase production of certain resources.
8. Utilize local seed sources and put high priority on natural regeneration processes.
9. Favor management actions that will allow the utilization of the valuable products that result from good management.
10. Avoid management treatments that fail to protect the unique values of the individual communities.
11. Copy Nature's Way by using silvicultural treatments that naturally regenerate new plants and communities.
12. Limit the use of prescribed fire to avoid the loss of valuable by-products and apply the treatment on an individual community basis.
13. Carefully weigh the environmental consequences of prescribed fire on the human environment.
14. Put even-age-management (clear-cutting), in the tool box with the other silvicultural tools, and apply only when it is the best tool to achieve your pre-established

goals. In other words, stop considering how to maximize the production of wood fiber per acre and, concentrate on forest health and diversity.

15. Above all else, get your potentially affected interests involved in establishing clear goals for the proposed project before considering how to accomplish the project. A mistake here can derail your whole effort.
16. Finally, keep your goal of healthy, vigorous, and diverse forest communities up front. Do not get sidetracked by some assigned target by the agency or company. Quality must win out!

Healthy diverse Northern Hardwood community

I continue to read and observe managers and decision makers frustrated by their inability to implement their proposed solutions to issues and problems. When I review the individual cases, I am seldom surprised to find major failures in communications with the potentially effected interests, which is resulting in objections and even lawsuits to stop the proposed action or solution. Trained decision makers can, definitely, improve their implementation success by studying "Citizen's Participation by Objective". Advanced education, after employment, in managerial skills and public involvement should be required for promotion to leadership positions.

It is apparent, that many of our politicians who refuse to accept the impact humans are having on our environment, are either intentionally ignoring or ignorant of the obvious facts identifying the current conditions of our natural surroundings. Empirical observation during one's life time, clearly establishes that much change has occurred just during the past 75 years of my life. During my early years, I took every opportunity to be on a trout stream casting a fly, or in the woods trying to out-smart the fox squirrel or the rabbit. I drank from the clear water in the streams, with no concern for pollution, and I swam in the crystal clear water of the inland lakes. Today I carry a ceramic filter to remove the toxins and germs from the creek water and I seldom enter the lake or even eat the fish from the lake. Even the fish from the clear water of the Great Lakes, are not suppose to be eaten too frequently due to toxins stored in the belly fat of the fish. There is almost no surface water on this planet that is safe to use without purification. I live on a small lake in the mid-west, and the lake association spends almost $200, 000.00 annually to treat the lake with poisons to kill the noxious weeds.

When I fly, I look down on the large cities and see a the haze hanging over the area and realize this is the air we are breathing. It has gotten so bad, I can see the pollution clouds even from a distance as I approach the urban areas by car.

I have photographed the land with deep gullies, called arroyos, which are the result of soil erosion. Lands that were once prairie lands with tall grass are now dry, baked areas with very limited vegetation and most of the top-soil washed away.

One simply cannot deny the changes that have occurred and are continually reducing the productivity of our natural world.

History clearly demonstrates the difficulty of implementing major changes and also shows us, these needed changes seldom come from the top down. The wealthy and powerful are comfortable and provided for so, why should they search for new ways? CEO's may be good at financial decisions, but seldom suggest ways to improve customer satisfaction. Methods to provide better service to meet customer demands or improve life styles, invariably, come from the bottoms up. Even politicians, who are elected public servants, responsible to the people, seldom solve important problems without strong pressure from the voter themselves. Changing the status quo happens when the dissatisfaction of the people demand the change.

Our forests are like a mosaic of individual communities with a multitude of relationships at work within each community. The remaining forested lands must be managed to keep them functioning at their optimal level, which means keeping them healthy and vigorous. Our management must work to rebuild the diversity that was natural in the beginning. If we truly care about future generations, we all have a job to do. It will matter little about your ancestral background or where you live today, for it will require working and sharing to complete this assignment. Diversity among the people is an asset to success, as the problem is worldwide. Together we can make a difference!

I can summarize this entire book in a short sentence, "YOU CANNOT PLANT A COMMUNITY FROM A SACK OF SEEDS". Trees alone do not a community make!

When I started, I thought I was writing a book about trees, I now realize this book is about people and their relationship to trees!

End Notes

1 Sullivan, John O. (1845) United States Magazine and Democratic Review, article entitled "Annexation."
2 Bryan, William Jennings (1899) "Republic or Empire."
3 Adams, Sean Patrick (2008) "The Early American Republic, A Documentary Reader."
4 History of Europe – Demographics and Agriculture (195896/ history of Europe/ 276190/ Demographics- and- Agriculture- growth 994290) Encyclopedia Britannica.
5 History of Europe – Demographics and Agriculture (195896/ history of Europe/ 276190/ Demographics- and- Agriculture- growth 994290) Encyclopedia Britannica.
6 Girardet, Herbert, "Save the Forests, Save the Planet," originally published in the Gaia Magazine, reprinted in the New Renaissance Magazine Vol. 2, No. 2.
7 USDA, Forest Service, 7/5/2007, Report on Abuse.
8 National Geographic, 1996, Effects of Deforestation, "Modern Day Plaque."
9 Experimental Forest: Implications for Sustainable Management of Hardwood Forests. U.S. Department of Agriculture, Forest Service, Northern Research Station.
10 National Geographic, 1996, Effects of Deforestation, "Modern Day Plaque."
11 United States Geological Survey, "Desertification." 1997.
12 Earth Policy Institute, (4/04/2006) "World Forests Continue to Shrink."
13 National Geographic, 1996, Effects of Deforestation, "Modern Day Plaque."
14 National Geographic, 1996, Effects of Deforestation, "Modern Day Plaque."
15 "World Population Prospects: The 2010 Revision Press Release."

16 Girardet, Herbert, "Save the Forests, Save the Planet," published in the Gaia Magazine, London and reprintein New Renaissance Magazine, Vol. 2, No. 2.

17 National Geographic, 1996 Effects of Deforestation, "Modern Day Plaque."

18 ScienceDaily, (Sept. 25, 2008), "Impact Of Beetle Kill On Rocky Mountain Weather, Air Quality."

19 Odum, E.P.: Barrett, G. W. (2005), "Fundamentals of Ecology."

20 Benson, K. R. (2000). "The Emergence of Ecology from Natural History."

21 Odum, E.P.; Barrett, G.W.; (2005), "Fundamentals of Ecology."

22 Liknes, Greg C., Nelson, Mark D., Butler, Brett J.,"Public and Private Forest Ownership in the Conerminous United States," Forest Resources of the United States, 2007, U.S. Department of Agriculture, Forest Service.

23 Michigan State University, Extension, Teachers Guide, "Forest Environment – A Healthy Forest."

24 Henderson, D., Krahl L., (1994), "Public Management Of Federal Forest Lands In The United States."

25 White Jr., Lynn Townsend, (1997) Journal of Science, "The Historical Roots of Our Ecologic Crisis."

26 White Jr., Lynn Townsend, (1997) Journal of Science, "The Historical Roots of Our Ecologic Crisis."

27 Kahneman, Danial, Nobel laureate, (2011), "Think Fast, Think Slow."

28 USDA, Forest Service (7/5/2007), "Report on Abuse."

29 Henderson, D., Krahl L., (1994), "Public Management Of Federal Forest Lands In The United States."

30 Seyyed Hossein Nasr, (1997), "Man and Nature: The Spiritual Crisis in Modern Man," Kazi Publishers.

31 Foltz, Richard, (2002), "Worldviews, Religion, and the Environment: A Global Anthology."

32 White Jr., Lynn Townsend, (1997), Journal of Science, "The Historical Roots of Our Ecologic Crisis."

33 Nesburn, Kent & Mengelkock, Louise, (1991), "Native American Wisdom."

34 Fitzgerald, Michael O. and Judith, (2003) "Indian Spirit" revised and enlarged.

35 Nesburn, Kent & Mengelkock, Louise, (1991), "Native American Wisdom."

36 White Jr., Lynn Townsend, (1997), Journal of Science, "The Historical Roots of Our Ecologic Crisis."

37 "L'Anse aux Meadows National Historic Site of Canada" (Parks Canada, 2007).

38 Govan, Fiona (2010-11-16). "First Americans' from Europe Five Centuries Before Columbus Voyages."

39 Brown, M.D., Hasseini, S.H., Torroni, A., Bendelt H.J., Allen, J.C., Schurr T.G., Scozzon, R., Cruciani F., Wallace, D.C., "An Ancient Link Between Europe/ Western Asia and North America?" American Journal of Human Genetics (Dec. 1998).

40 "History of Europe – Demographic and Agricultural Growth," Encyclopedia Britannica.

41 Goldsmith, James L., (1995), "The Crisis Of The Late Middle Ages: The Case of France."

42 Morison, Samuel Elliot, "Admiral Of The Ocean Sea: The Life of Christopher Columbus." (1942).

43 Hoxie, Frederic E., Encyclopedia of North American Indians, (March 1997).

44 Taylor, Alan, (2002), American Colonies: Volume I Of The Penquin History of The United States: History of The United States Series.

45 Winship, George Parker, "The Journey of Coronado, 1540-1542 From The City of Mexico to The Grand Canyon of The Colorado and The Buffalo Plains of Texas, Kansas, and Nebraska, As Told by Himself and His Followers, A.S. Barnes & Co. (1904).

46 Nesburn, Kent & Mengelkoch, Louise, (1991), "Native American Wisdom."

47 Thornton, Russell,(1990), "American Indian Holocaust and Survival: a population history since 1492, University of Oklahoma Press.

48 Nesburn, Kent & Mengelkoch, Louise, M.A., (1991) "Native American Wisdom."

49 Nesburn, Kent & Mengelkoch, Louise, (1991), "Native American Wisdom."

50 Nesburn, Kent & Mengelkoch, Louise, (1991), "Native American Wisdom."

51 Burnett, Edward Cody, (1941), "The Continental Congress," New York.

52 Christie and Labaree, "Empire or Independence," and Boyd, Julian P., (1945), The Declaration of Independence; The Revolution of the Text."

53 Koschmann, A.H. and Bergendahl, (1968), "Principle Gold-Producing Districts of the United States," U.S. Geological Survey, Professional Paper 610.

54 Edgar, Wesley Owen, (1975), "Treck of the Oil Finders" American Association of Petroleum Geologists.

55 Nerburn, Kent, Mengelkoch, Louise, (1991), "Native American Wisdom."

56 Wilkinson, Charles F., (1992), "Crossing the Next Meridian: Land, Water, and the Future of the West." Island Press.

57 Wilkinson, Charles F., (1992), "Crossing the Next Meridian: Land, Water, and the Future of the West." Island Press.

58 Wilkinson, Charles F., (1992), Crossing the Next Meridian: Land, Water, and the Future of the West," Island Press.

59 Pratt, Julius, (July 1927), "The Origin Of Manifest Destiny," American Historical Review; O'Sullivan, John L.,(1845), "Annexation" and "A Divine Destiny for American."

60 Schurz, Carl, "The Reminiscences of Carl Shurz," Vol. I.

61 The Senate of the University of Toronto, 1923, Dr. B. E. Fernow —An Appreciation of his Services.

62 Twight, B. W., (1990) "Bernard Fernow and Prussian Forestry in America."

63 Goldsmith, James L., (1995), "The Crisis Of The Middle Ages: The Case Of France."

64 Twight, B. W., (1990), "Bernard Fernow and Prussian Forestry in America."

65 Davis, Richard C., (September 29, 2005), "National Forests of the United States," The Forest History Society.

66 Schenck, Carl Alwin, "Cradle of Forestry in America; The Biltmore Forest School introduction by Steven Anderson (1998).

67 Cradle of Forestry in America: The Biltmore Forest School, 1898-1913.

68 Cradle of Forestry in America: The Biltmore Forest School, 1898-1913.

69 Noble Jr., Ransom E., (1976), "Pinchot, Gifford," In William D. Halsey. Collier's Encyclopedia 19.

70 Lewis, James G. (1999), "The Pinchot Family and the Battle to Establish American Forestry."

71 "The History of Forestry in America," Yearbook of Agriculture, 1949, Washington D.C.

72 "The History of Forestry in America," Yearbook of Agriculture, 1949, Washington D.C.

73 Ponder, Stephen, (1987), "Gifford Pinchot, Press Agent for Forestry," Journal of Forest History 31.

74 McGeary, M. Nelson, (1960), "Gifford Pinchot: Forester-Politician."

75 Noble Jr., Ransom E. (1976), "Pinchot, Gifford." In William D. Halsey. Collier's Encyclopedia. 19.

76 Pinchot, Gifford, "Brett Burnett, Edward Cody, (1941), "The Continental Congress," New York. Breaking New Ground," Harcourt Brace Jovanovich, 1947. In print, 1998, by Island Press.

77 Davis, Richard C., (Sept. 29, 2005), "National Forests of the United States," The Forest History Society.

78 Pinchot, Gifford, (1947) "Breaking New Ground."

79 Pinchot, Gifford, (1947), "Breaking New Ground."

80 McGeary, M. Nelson, (1960), "Gifford Pinchot Forester – Politician."

81 U.S. Forest Service History, William B. Greeley, Third Chief, 1920-1928.

82 U.S. Forest Service History, "Establishment of Forest Reserves and Land Status Change," The Forest History Society.

83 Economic Research Service / USDA, (2002), "Major Uses of Land in the United States."

84 Davis, Richard C., (Sept. 29, 2005), "National Forests of the United States," The Forest History Society.

85 Meine, (1987), "Aldo Leopold: His Life and Work."

86 Merrill, Perry H., (1981), "Roosevelts Forest Army: A History of the Civilian Conservation Corps."

87 U S D A, Forest Service, "Road Management Website."

88 Sadler, Russell, (July 24, 2005), "Real Healthy Forests," Blue Oregon, blueoregon.com.

89 "World Population Prospects: The 2010 Revision Press Release," Population Division of the Department of Economic and Social Affairs of the United Nations Secretariat, May 2011.

90 Noss, R. F. (1990), "Indicators for Monitoring Biodiversity: A Hierarchical Approach."

91 CitiLog, Leader in Upcycling and Repurposing of Trees Into Finished Wood Products, "Wood Chips, Mulch & The Release Of Carbon Dioxide." Also, Obey Mother Nature, "North American Hardwoods Produce Oxygen: Store Carbon," obeymothernature.com.

92 Dr. Franklin, Jerry, U. S. Forest Service scientist and The College of Natural Resources, University of Washington.

93 Bleiker, Hans, Doctorate Thesis, "Augmentation and Meta Process: A Strategy for Responsive and Responsible Decision Making by Public Officials," Massachusetts Institute of Technology, 1972.